the OX
and the ASS

Escaping Toxic-Relationship Dynamics

the OX
and the ASS

MICHAEL A. CAPARRELLI
PhD (abd)

Published by UNMUTED Publications

Visit: unmuted.app
Contact: unmuted777@gmail.com

Back Cover Photo: Rebecca Daniele
(Facebook: *Radiance by Rebecca Photography*)
Cover Concept: Sarah Vass

Book Design: wordsintheworks.com

A specially-formatted workbook is available
online to accompany this book.

Please join our OX & ASS *club* at Facebook.com/mcaparrelli

ALSO BY MICHAEL A. CAPARRELLI

~

Pen Your Pain Into Parables
A TOOL FOR RECOVERY
See Page 155

To Alicia,
a true OX in every sense of the word.
I love you.

Foreword by

Judge Elizabeth Ortiz Whited

My name is Elizabeth Ortiz Whited. I am a practicing family court attorney in the State of Rhode Island as well as the first Hispanic female judge on the municipal level in Rhode Island. To most, my professional accomplishments and accolades paints the picture of someone who was able to stay the course and accomplish everything she pursued, but underneath all my professional success is a story of a wounded child who had to navigate and work through difficult experiences, emotions and memories to be able to write this foreword.

You see, for most of my life, I came to accept chaos as my norm. As a child of immigrant parents, I was constantly exposed to the stressors that come with living in financial and emotional uncertainty. Memories of my childhood are inundated with fights about finances, adultery and substance abuse. As a result, I became parentified at a very young age and felt an overwhelming sense of responsibility for my mother's and my siblings' safety. Consequently, I lacked the emotional support necessary to have any confidence in myself or my environment.

Being exposed to constant chaos led to me finding refuge in school and my academic performance as those were the only arenas where I felt safe enough to thrive. My obsession with being a good student left my emotional development on the back burner, which ultimately led to my inability to trust my instincts when it came to interpersonal relationships. As a result, I found myself engaged in toxic adult relationships and constant confusion as to why someone as bright as myself could find herself trapped in webs of dysfunction. Perhaps you too have lived a contradictory life where you flourish in certain areas such as your vocation but find yourself stuck in other areas such as your intimate relationships.

Despite those dysfunctional interpersonal relationships, God gave me the strength and courage to continue pursuing my education which eventually led to a law degree and successful career as a Family Law attorney. Oftentimes people would ask me why I chose such an emotionally draining area of law to commit my life to. I never really had an answer until I dug deep into my own brokenness and found myself trusting in God and seeking a deeper spiritual connection with Him. The more I delved into the issues that kept families trapped in toxic cycles, the more I realized that my work in Family Law brought me better understanding of my tendency and even willingness to be an Ox in my relationships.

With the help of books like, *"The Ox and the Ass"* and *"Pen Your Pain Into Parables"*, as well as regular therapy and a deeper connection with God, I was finally able to surrender to the idea that I am good enough. Not only am I good enough, I have been able to grow through the emotional damage that my childhood caused me. That growth has allowed me to believe, albeit in very small increments, that I am deserving of love, support and oxen in my life.

As a family law attorney, I am constantly exposed to clients and families who are trapped in toxic situations. Those situations are often the result of dysfunctional patterns of behavior that are deep rooted. As a court appointed Guardian Ad Litem, I often witness how generational curses can affect children and how they view the world. The anger, resentment and negative feelings that their parents feel for each other are the main causes of stress for most of those children and often they do not have a safe "pen" to retreat to.

My goal as a Guardian Ad Litem is to assist those families and the Courts in finding the supports that the families need, typically in the form of mediation, mental health services and even a referee (yes, I obtained a Juris Doctorate to referee fighting parents). My hope is that by the time the case is resolved in the court system, that the parents are able to identify the ways in which their children are negatively impacted by their toxic behavior as well as identifying ways to help their children cope through their parents' separation/divorce.

Toxic-relationships are not limited to any socio-economic class, race, gender or religion. Reading the Ox and the Ass will help you through the shame and guilt that often keeps us trapped in toxic-relationships. For me, finding a supportive church community (Pastor Mike was my first pastor), trustworthy friends and activities that reignite your soul saved my life. This book will help you identify ways to take control of your life in the midst of feeling like you are powerless. There is hope for your situation, but that hope starts with you. The Ox and the Ass is a good place to start in identifying the ways in which you can change your life and the way you see yourself.

Foreword by

Pasco A. Manzo

President of Adult & Teen Challenge New England and New Jersey

Ephesians 3:20 says, "Now to him who is able to do immeasurably more than all we ask or imagine, according to his power that is at work within us, to him be glory in the church and in Christ Jesus throughout all generations, for ever and ever!"

Over 43 years ago, I committed myself to serve Jesus Christ and walk in His plan for my life. Over the past four decades, I've seen countless people's lives saved by the power of God and His Word. I've witnessed so many miracles during 25 years of pastoring, sitting on various ministry boards, being a victim's advocate, traveling the world, and now serving as President of Adult &Teen Challenge New England & New Jersey, a worldwide faith-based substance abuse treatment program.

At Adult & Teen Challenge, lives are transformed from the grips of addiction. How does this happen? First, by prioritizing a personal relationship with Jesus Christ above and beyond any other human relationship. Secondly, supportive spouses, significant others and family plays the strongest role as they understand the importance of a strong walk with God as priority and come alongside of the Teen Challenge loved-one with the same faith that God can do all things. Healthy relationships are one of the keys to sobriety.

One of the phenomenons I've have seen frequently are those

who are in unhealthy relationships vacillating and relapsing when endeavoring to get healthy and free from their life controlling problems. Unfortunately, unhealthy people attract unhealthy people only to diminish the capacity to dream again. Then if they marry and divorce, the divorce rate for second marriages is 67-80%. Why, because most people unconsciously replicate their prior spouses simply because they are "drawn" to that type of person.

Yet as we place these unhealthy relationships before the altar of God and surrender all, the result is CHANGED LIVES. Teen Challenge New England & New Jersey has several book compilations of miraculous stories of those people who were either addicted to drugs, alcohol, and/or have strained or even destroyed relationships of all kinds and without hope and then encounter the living God and find HOPE in Jesus Christ the Savior of the world and the Teen Challenge Program! Can you and your spouse and/or loved one become free from the control of addiction and live a productive life together? Absolutely yes! God has a plan for you too!

If you are a single person looking for Mr. or Mrs. Right, read "The Ox and the Ass" first in order to get to know yourself and avoid making future mistakes. Also, if you are in recovery and struggling in a very difficult and abusive relationship, this book may be an encouragement to you. Remember, as Ephesians 3:20 above says, you too can achieve things beyond your dreams with the help of God.

Breaking Soul Ties

She smiles,
Not because he treats her so right
Empty vases, distant dinners, bitter fights.
She smiles, Because the kids are in sight.

She serves,
Not because he gave her so much.
Wasted cash, lap dances, angry touch
She serves, Because it's what she does.

She stays,
Not because he's been a good man.
Oxytocin, guilt trips, Bible commands
She stays, Because there's no feasible plan.

She leaves,
Not because she wants her fun.
Barren days, hate mirrors, coming undone.
She leaves, because she despises who she's become.

Finally....

She's at peace,
Not because she's found her guy.
Budding flowers, soothing flutes, lakeside.
She's at peace,
Because she's broken the tie.

–*Michael A. Caparrelli*

INTRODUCTION

In a culture of individualism, the quality of your life depends upon *who* you are. You've heard it echoed a gazillion ways in songs, books, films and memes: *"Happiness is an inside job."*

The sages of the age preach that your life-satisfaction hinges on what happens within your own mind. According to contemporary gurus, your fulfillment is a result of what transpires between your ears. Factors such as your mental outlook, emotional health, genetical makeup, and physical shape all play critical functions in determining your happiness. Once again, according to the experts of our era, the quality of your life all hinges on *who* you are.

What if I told you that your sobriety, sanity and success hinges not only on who you are, but *whose* you are?

In other words, your life-satisfaction depends upon the caliber of covenants you establish with partners, lovers, friends and mentors.

What if I told you that your *vibe* is partly resultant from your *tribe*? If you feel bad vibes, it could be because you belong to a toxic tribe.

So, before you diagnose yourself as mentally ill, make sure you aren't just surrounded by whack-jobs. Your well-being is not merely the result of your intellections but also your interactions. Let's back up this notion with some scientific and theological evidence.

Regarding your sobriety, a study from the 1970's known as the *Rat Park Experiment* confirms that your relationships keep you strong in your war against substance temptation. Within this experiment, Canadian psychologist Bruce K. Alexander designed a large housing colony 200 times the size of a laboratory cage for a group of rats to live within community. In addition, the scientists designed cages for another group of rats to live within isolation.

Both groups of rats—the socialized and the isolated—were given the option of drinking from two different dispensers. One dispenser held sweetened morphine while the other dispenser contained plain tap water.

In short, the socialized rats preferred tap water while the isolated rats favored morphine. It was inferred by researchers that the socialized rats were already fulfilled from their social bonds; therefore, less susceptible to morphine temptation. The conclusion of this experiment is that the fulfillment from your social connections rein in your appetite for substance abuse.

Conversely, the wrong social connections play a role in your demise. Some mistakenly suppose that Adam bit the forbidden fruit in the garden of Eden to please himself. In Genesis 3, God tells Adam that the reason he fell from grace was because he "listened to the voice of the woman."

Therefore, Adam did *not* indulge the forbidden fruit to please himself; he indulged it to please his wife. Adam is a case-study where a man falls into temptation, not because of his intellections, but because of his interactions. Adam is an example of how toxic-relationships can sabotage your sobriety.

In 2001, researchers Fals-Stewart, O'Farrell and Hooley published their findings from a quantitative study in *Behavior Therapy Academic Journal* that indicated a correlation between perceived criticism from a spouse and relapse into substance abuse.

Data collected from participants within the study showed that they were able to maintain sobriety for shorter periods of time within relationships where they felt judged or merely critiqued.

Who knows? Perhaps Eve browbeat Adam to the point where he was willing to defy the very commands of God.

Whether we are talking about the Rat Park Experiment or Adam & Eve, both cases demonstrate that your well-being hinges not solely on *who* you are but also *whose* we are. Take heed to the covenants you form!

Interestingly enough, in a survey that I (as a PhD candidate in Behavioral Science) conducted amongst the residents of both Massachusetts and Greater Boston Teen Challenge's Substance Abuse Treatment Programs, it was found that *Relationship Problems* were the number one concern as a potential trigger for relapse.

Along with relationship problems, the survey offered the options of financial problems, peer pressure, criminal background related issues and mental health issues. The residents attested to the fact that their covenants with lovers, family and friends were the greatest potential stumbling block on their road to recovery.

Even if you have no substance abuse issues, how many times have you devoured a carton of Ben and Jerry's Ice Cream, or eaten your way through five bags of Doritos after a lovers-quarrel?

Regarding your sanity, a 2015 survey about the mental health of children and adolescents indicated that relationships were the single greatest risk factor in triggering neurosis. Issues like depression and anxiety were most often provoked by times spent with friends and family. No wonder why the great philosopher of our day, Danny DeVito stated, *"Happiness is having a large, loving family that lives in another state."*

Make no mistake about it: so much of your mood hinges on the quality of people with whom you reside.

Regarding your success, a study conducted by Olivet Nazarene University showed that 76% of people express the importance of mentor-relationships within their life. The same study indicated that folks with mentors are far happier within their careers than folks without mentors.

Once again, the premise of this book is confirmed—the quality of your life hinges not merely on *who* you are but *whose* you are.

Now, simpletons argue that being in covenant with the wrong people is better than being in covenant with no people. In other words, company is better than isolation even if it's the wrong company. According to the wisest man that ever lived, King Solomon, that kind of thinking is what they call in the 12-step community, *stinking-thinking*. King Solomon tells us in Proverbs 21:19: *"Better to live alone in a desert than with a quarrelsome spouse."* Being a pastor of many people for sixteen years, I can attest to the fact that the perils of loneliness are a mere fleabite in comparison to the chaos of being in a contentious relationship. While I pray that God sends you the right people to love and lead you, rest assured that...

It would be better for you to die not having what you want than die having what you don't want.

By claiming that your life-satisfaction hinges on your interactions equally as much as your intellections, let me make it clear that I am *not* promoting an external locus of control. In psychology, an external locus of control is the idea that the outcomes of your life are resultant from factors outside of you.

Folks with an external locus of control blame people, places, and things for their well-being rather than taking personal responsibility. Folks with an external locus of control play the victim to circumstances, forever crying, "it's not my fault."

Instead, what I'm arguing is an internal locus of control whereby you take responsibility for the choices you make within your relationships such as who you bond with.

Now, if there are any toxic-relationships in your life, if there are any unequal yokes (a.k.a. the OX and the ASS), it is a tango between two parties that involves the participation of both.

It would be easy to convict the *narcissist* alone for such a blood-sucking relationship. However, according to Dr. Rachel Negar Partiali, the relationship between the *narcissist* and the *empath* is a dance that involves both participants. If the *empath* walks off the dance floor at any point (after coming to their senses), the music might not stop right away but the dance will at least be finished. Facts are, the *empath* keeps dancing. Facts are, the toxic tango continues because of the *empath's* deep-seated mindsets that keep them grooving to the beat. Until those mindsets are confronted, mended and reformed, the dangerous dance continues.

If you are an OX mating with an ASS, or are inclined to do so, this book will help you break free from unequaled yokes.

There are two lenses through which you can interpret this book: *prevention* or *intervention.*

If you're a single person with few relationships in your life, you can read this book through the lens of *prevention.* May the wisdom from this book spare you from establishing toxic-relationships with ASSES (a term you will comprehend better as you read further into this book) that deplete all your energy and sabotage your success.

If you're an OX that's already mated with an ASS (or vice versa) within marriage or other kinds of relationships, you could read this book through the lens of *intervention*. May this book empower you to make decisions that redirect your relationships down a healthier path.

Or, in some cases, especially where perpetual abuse, addiction, adultery and abandonment are present within the relationship—*The Four Circles* are discussed a little later—may this book help you make a successful break from such a toxic bond.

Just to be clear about the terms, *empath* and *narcissist*. *Empaths* are nurturing individuals inclined to *"do good"* towards their fellow humans where *narcissists* are self-aggrandizing egomaniacs who only care to *"look good."*

My pastor, Pasco Manzo, would use the idioms, *LMs* (Low-Maintenance) and *HMs* (High-Maintenance) in depicting people who don't ask for much yet give continually (*LMs*), and those who would suck the blood from a leech for survival (*HMs*).

Of course, these monikers are over-simplifications in describing the multi-faceted nature of homo sapiens. Few people are purely empathetic or narcissistic; rather, in the words of Oswald Chambers, *"In every person, there is a potential hero and a skunk."* Or, as the Apostle Paul states in the New Testament, we all have *"a spirit and a flesh."*

Nonetheless, we sometimes find ourselves playing a certain role in relationships whereas our partner party plays the counterpart. While this role may not capture who we are in totality, we play it wholeheartedly within certain contexts. In some relationships, we assume the role of Empath (a.k.a., the OX) whereas our partner plays the Narcissist (a.k.a. the ASS). Sooner or later, these unholy alliances undermine every area of our life until we end up on psychiatric drugs, drinking our sorrows away with copious amounts of vodka or emotionally detaching from life. If you find yourself trapped in one of these unholy alliances, or have a history of doing so, this book is for you. In reading this book, you will explore the following questions:

- Am I an OX mating with an ASS?
- What keeps me stuck within this relationship?
- How is this relationship affecting my sanity, sobriety and success?
- What are the specific decisions I must make to break free from this yoke?
- What should I anticipate as I make these decisions?
- What does a healthy relationship look like?

The following pages offer lots of scientific evidence, inspirational examples from the Bible, along with the testimonies of multiple people who escaped toxic-relationship dynamics. Some testimonies are from folks who reached a *bend in the road* within their relationships whereby they made decisions to redirect their relationship down a healthier path. Others reached the *end of the road* whereby they had to leave for their own safety. Whether you are an OX or an ASS, male or female, old or young, single or married, may this book set the tone for healthier relationships within your life.

Please note: if you or someone you know is a victim of domestic violence, the **National Domestic Violence Hotline** can help. The number is 1-800-799-7233.

CHAPTER ONE
Going in Circles

"Do not plow with an ox and an ass
yoked together" (Deuteronomy 22:10).

THE OX AND THE ASS

When a farmer makes the mistake of yoking the liveliest animal with the laziest animal on the farm—the OX and the ASS—a relationship between two incompatible creatures is established. True to its reputation, the OX is an industrious beast that bears its load with grit and grace.

On the contrary, the ASS is a sluggish animal that contributes little on the farm while consuming a lot.

The OX is a cooperative animal that does whatever is required, whereas the ASS is too stubborn to venture beyond its own comfort and convenience.

Such a striking dissimilarity of character!

No surprise whatsoever that the Bible warns against forging such a mismatched union in Deuteronomy 22:10, where it says, "Do not plow with an ox and ass yoked together."

God knows that…

For two creatures to have a relationship that's amicable, their character must be compatible.

When you met your mate, the vibes between the two of you sparked a spell-binding chemistry that you could not resist. Perhaps you were from Yale and he was from jail, and the romance began.

Or maybe she was a little rough around the edges, you delighted in a good challenge, and the "law of opposites attract" prevailed.

In the beginning, the contrast between the two of you kept you on the edge of your seat. Fast forward several years and the differences between the two of you pushed you to the edge of a cliff.

Some differences between two people in a union are fantastic, resulting in a lifetime of intellectual intrigue and erotic love. On the other hand, other differences are a matter of light and darkness, resulting in years of headaches and heartache.

Could you yourself be in a relationship where an OX is mating with an ASS?

Let's continue to see if you are in such a mismatched union.

When an OX mates with an ASS, the OX works tirelessly shouldering all of its obligatory loads.

Perhaps you relate to the OX, being the caliber of person who offers 100% to your commitments.

In your romantic relationship, maybe you plan the dates, buy gifts, make dinner, offer compliments and/or show continual affection.

Like the OX, you are not just involved but invested in your relationship.

As the OX works feverishly, the ASS sprawls out on the farm without a care in the world. The union between the lively and the lazy produces a tiring, tragic dynamic.

Given the fact that the ASS is nothing more than dead weight, the OX makes very little headway in its work while its yoked to the ASS.

Lots of the OX's energy is squandered—not moving forward, but going in circles.

Get this picture in your mind—a hardworking animal, yoked to a loafer animal, slowly losing its stamina from going in circles.

Are you in a relationship that's going in circles?

The Profile of an OX

- If you're sensitive to the needs of others, you might be an OX.
- If you enjoy serving more than being served, you might be an OX.
- If you easily take responsibility for others' issues, you might be an OX.
- If you initiate most of what happens in your relationships, you might be an OX.
- If you perceive your sacrifices for others as a privilege, you might be an OX.
- If disloyalty or dishonesty crushes you, you might be an OX.
- If you are generous with your time, talents and resources, you might be an OX.
- If you have the potential of being an enabler/codependent, you might be an OX.
- If you're drawn to ASSES (as described below), you might be an OX.

The Profile of an ASS

- If you're a habitual offender with one of the Four A Circles (described below), you might be an ASS.
- If you have a propensity to blame others for what's wrong, you might be an ASS.
- If you hate being inconvenienced or going out of your way, you might be an ASS.
- If you are defensive about your defects, you might be an ASS.

- If your closed to the idea of therapy regarding your issues, you might be an ASS.
- If you lack the energy to invest in your relationship, you might be an ASS.
- If you mull over your own feelings more than others, you might be an ASS.
- If you are drawn to OXEN (as described above), you might be an ASS.

Why are OXEN attracted to ASSES?

In Deuteronomy 22:10 prohibits farmers from yoking an OX and with an ASS, then it stands to reason that this was a common mistake made on the farm. Imperatives are typically given in areas where we are tempted to do the opposite of what's being commanded. For instance, we would never be commanded to not look at a person lustfully if it wasn't our proclivity to do so. The command itself insinuates the reality of farmers making this foolish mistake on the regular.

If farmers had the habit of yoking OXEN with ASSES, for what reason would they yoke such contrary creatures? I'm no agriculturalist but I would imagine the farmer assuming that the OX could help the ASS become a better animal. Perhaps the OX could bring out the very best in the ASS, reforming the lazy animal into a lively animal.

But Moses, operating in divine wisdom, issues the command knowing that it will not work out the way that the farmer presumed.

Instead, the ASS will become even lazier knowing he can ride on the strength of the OX. In other words, the animal will just take advantage of the OX's benevolent nature. In summary, the two of them will go in circles rather than going forward.

Isn't this an accurate explanation behind your attraction to ASSES? You actually believe that you can reform your ASS into a better person.

Maybe you believe that your love is powerful enough to transform them into someone with better morals, ethics and principles.

But what you discover is the opposite—a yoke with an ASS makes you *lesser* far easier than you make them *better!*

You become lesser spiritually, emotionally and financially from going in constant circles.

Let me break it down for you like this. If you stand on top of a table while your ASS sits in a chair, and you're both pulling at each other, the law of gravity teaches us that the ASS will yank you down far easier than you will pull them up!

That same law applies in a relational context. Make no mistake about it...

An ASS will make you lesser far quicker and easier than you will make them better!

The Four "A" Circles

Consider the following circles you make when you're an OX married to an ASS. You could be a male OX mating with a female ASS, or a female OX mating with a male ASS. Either way, these are the kinds of circles that characterize spiritually incompatible relationships.

If you feel dizzy from being with your mate, you might be an OX yoked to an ASS, caught up in one or more of these circles.

The Circle of Addiction

You surmise that your partner is using again. Disappearing acts, drained bank accounts, dilated eyes, dramatic personality changes and countless other signs all hint towards substance abuse. You confront your partner. Not only do they deny such an allegation, but they lash out at you for not trusting them. You tell yourself to "quit being a nag." And so you invalidate your gut instinct as being your own craziness and let the whole thing go. You fall prey to the gaslighting tactics that addicts employ so masterfully.

Then a crisis of some sort startles you like being shaken out of a deep sleep. A phone call from the police, a scream from the other room, a head-on collision with the family car or some other catastrophe yanks you out of your denial.

Caught in flagrante delicto, your partner has no choice but to admit they have a problem. Of course, they start in-patient or out-patient treatment for a substance abuse disorder, start attending 12-step meetings or become more involved in church, all because they are scared of losing you.

But, within a short time, your partner relapses. According to the American Addiction Center, between 40-60% of all people with a substance abuse disorder will relapse after starting a recovery program.

And the merry-go-round of mayhem continues for another ten, fifteen, twenty and even thirty years.

The Circle of Adultery

Like noticing the atmospheric changes that occur when a season ends while introducing another, you discern deviations from the norm in your relationship. Perhaps you notice several of the signs listed below, all possible indications of an extramarital affair published by *Psychology Today*.

1. Your partner makes radical improvements in their physical appearance.
2. Your partner becomes secretive about their phone or computer usage.
3. Your partner is unreachable for periods of time.
4. Your partner desires significantly less, more or different kinds of sex.
5. Your partner becomes hostile towards you and critical of the relationship.
6. Your partner alters their work schedule.
7. Your partner's friends are uncomfortable around you.
8. Your partner makes unexplainable financial expenses.
9. Your partner becomes emotionally unavailable.
10. Your partner deflects, avoids and/or gaslights every time you ask questions.

Finally, after being kissed for months with lies, the truth slaps you in the face!

You unearth a love letter buried in their work bag, or maybe you catch your partner having a tickle-party with a stranger.

To the degree of evidence that proves their guilt is to the same degree of truth to which they confess.

In other words, their admission of guilt never goes beyond the data you have at hand.

Of course, they exhibit a semblance of remorse while promising it will never happen again.

But, within a certain period of time, your partner returns to the same affair or begins a new rendezvous, proving the statistics to be true that people who cheat are three and a half times more likely to mess around again than those who have never cheated before (from a study published in *Psychology Today*).

And the loops continue while you become loopier.

The Circle of Abuse

In 1979, psychologist and leader in the field of Domestic Abuse, Lenore Edna Walker, conceptualized a theory that sheds light on the patterns of abuse in a relationship known as the Social Cycle Theory.

Within this theory, she laid out the following stages of abuse that happen almost as predictably as nightfall.

Stage 1: The Tension

Tension surges while the channel of communication closes between partners.

As the tension builds, the victimized partner becomes fearful and feels the need to appease the abusive partner.

Stage 2: The Incident

An episode of abuse erupts through verbal, physical and emotional abuse. Accompanying the abuse, there is also anger, blaming, arguing, threats and intimidation.

Stage 3: The Reconciliation

The abusive partner apologizes, gives excuses, blames the victim, denies or minimizes the abuse and/or promises that he or she will never do it again.

Stage 4: *The Calm*

With the incident being almost forgotten, the couple slips into a blissful period of perceiving their relationship through rose-colored glasses.

When you're stuck in a circle of abuse, these stages make loops for years without you even realizing their predictability. Each time, you somehow convince yourself that it will never happen again, yet you repeatedly prove yourself to be a false prophet. In many cases, the severity of the abuse escalates resultant from the sense of immunity that the abusive partner experiences as a result of never facing consequences.

The Circle of Abandonment

Your relationship becomes a game of cat and mouse. Your partner withdraws from you, which then elicits your pursuit for them. It is the old cliché, "you want what you can't have." The more your partner retreats, the greater your effort becomes to win their approval, affection or attention. The withdrawal might involve the deprivation of physical affection, verbal praise, sexual intercourse, mere attention, financial support or even their presence. You might play the game of cat and mouse for years while never catching more than a handful of fur. Below, you will find several forms of emotional abandonment:

- Deprived expression (the right to be heard)
- Deprived affection (the right to be physically nurtured)
- Deprived appreciation (the right to be verbally praised)
- Deprived respect (the right to be treated with dignity and value)
- Deprived time (the right of your presence)

Your partner may be conscious of these ploys, manipulatively using negative reinforcement tactics to control you. If these behaviors are a calculated ploy, you are likely dealing with someone who suffers from a personality disorder such as Narcissism or Borderline Personality. Or they may be unconscious of it all, simply behaving according to their own deficiency.

They simply cannot give you what they never received themselves.

It is called the Circle of Abandonment because the underlying fear that perpetuates the cycle is the fear of being forsaken by your partner. Every time they withhold something dear from you, it feels like the foreshadow of them leaving you once and for all. Under the constant threat of abandonment, you run yourself ragged trying to procure your partner's love and commitment. This circle keeps you stuck in a state of anxiety rather than the security that healthy relationships offer.

Let me break it down for you like this.

Once upon a time, a city boy moved to the country. During his first week on the farm, he was awakened at three in the morning by the sound of his neighbor's cock crowing.

For weeks, the city boy tossed and turned all throughout the night because of the crowing of the cock. After being fed up, he knocked on his neighbor's door and said, 'Every night, I lose hours of sleep because of the crowing of your cock!"

The neighbor replied, "That's impossible. He doesn't crow every night, and when he does crow, it's for only a minute or so."

The city boy responded, "Yes, but I spend the entire night waiting for the cock to crow."

When you are stuck in a circle of abandonment, you live many days under the threat of your partner's abandonment. You have such little tranquility because you spend most of your time anticipating the crowing of the cock. In other words, you live in the anticipation of them walking out the door.

Should I stay or should I go?

If you live in an unequally yoked marriage, you probably questioned many times, "Should I stay or should I go?"

Apart from folks in life-threatening situations, this is not an easy decision to make.

If you are a Christian, part of what makes this such a hard decision are all of the pro-marriage, anti-divorce scriptures in the Bible such as Malachi 2:16, Matthew 5:32, and I Corinthians 7:13. No question, these verses should inspire us to pause before flippantly deserting a sacred union.

In our day and age, the easiest term to throw around in a marriage is the D word. In the last few decades, it has become not only acceptable but oddly in vogue to get a divorce. In a metropolitan city in the US, a billboard hanging from a building sponsored by an attorney says, "Life is short. Be happy and get a divorce!" Sadly, because of this cultural trend, we have seen the percentage of fleeting marriages more than quadruple over the last few decades. Currently, almost half of all couples who say, "I do" will eventually say, "I'm done." Within that percentage, it stands to reason that some (*not* all) folks bailed from a broken relationship that could have been salvaged simply because it was the trendy thing to do.

In answering this difficult question—"Should I stay or should I go?"—there are way too many variables for a *one-size-fits-all* answer. This is a matter that cannot be determined by simply reading this book, but only resolved within your relationship with God as well as the spiritually mature people in your life. In some cases, it would be wise to run for the hills! But, in other cases, it would be prudent to tie a knot and hang on to the end of your rope!

State or Trait?

After facilitating sixteen years of marital counseling, I can attest to the fact that most relationships exhibit one or more of the states I described within the chapter—addiction, adultery, abuse, abandonment. Given the fact that we are all sinful human beings, struggling with dysfunctional proclivities even after a radical salvation experience, most couples will fall into one of these states periodically (hopefully, on the least severe side of the spectrum). One of the factors that determines whether you should stay or go hinges on whether these states have become traits; a *state* is a temporary window of time that elapses whereas a *trait* is a defining characteristic of your relationship. Have you visited these places here and there, or have they become circles you make over and over? Are these circles a state you've passed through, or have they become a trait that defines your relationship?

Sneak peak of what's ahead

So, what keeps a person stuck in this kind of relationship? If we were answering that question in the context of animals—like an OX and an ASS—we would reply with the term, Yoke. A Yoke is an apparatus that links the necks of two animals together, making it impossible for them to detach from one another. The Bible employs the metaphor of a yoke to describe all sorts of enslavements (Genesis 27:40, Isaiah 9:4-7, 10:27 and Matthew 11:30). In the next chapter, we will elaborate on the Yokes that grip a person's soul within a toxic-relationship, often making it feel impossible for them to break free from such a mismatched union.

CHAPTER TWO
The Yokes

"Be ye not yoked together with unbelievers;
for what fellowship has righteousness with unrighteousness.
And what communion has light with darkness"
(II Corinthians 6:14).

LOVE ADDICTION

Make no mistake about it, you can be addicted to *love* just as realistically as being hooked to a chemical substance. In fact, the chemicals triggered within your brain by your beloved's sight, scent or sound are just as intoxicating as any opioid, alcohol or other substance.

It is arguable that love is the most mind-altering, non-pharmaceutical narcotic, causing you to stay places longer than you want to stay, and making you pay prices you would never want to pay.

Consider the words of R&B singer from yesteryear, Percy Sledge, in his song, "When a Man Loves a Woman."

Notice how much his own love-addiction costs him; a high-price for such a low-life…

When a man loves a woman…can't keep his mind on nothin' else…he'd trade the world…or a good thing he's found.

Perhaps you're thinking, "I detest my partner and all the damage they do to me, so I couldn't possibly be addicted to them."

Be not deceived.

You don't have to enjoy something to be hooked to it. It is usually only in the beginning phases of an addiction that it's something you adore, eventually morphing into something you abhor. All addictions start out as something *"I get to do"*

39

eventually mutating into something *"I've got to do."*

Facts are, as much as you don't respect, enjoy or even desire your partner, if you can't get away from them, consider yourself *hooked* to them.

The real test to determine if something has a hold on you is to see how successful you are at resisting it.

A dog does not know his own bondage until he tries to escape from the leash.

Rumor has is it that contemporary singer, Rihanna, penned "Love on the Brain" about her co-dependent relationship to a physically abusive boyfriend.

The lyrics of the song show a woman desperate for a dangerous love, a relationship that she can't get away from, yet she can't seem to get enough of. The lyrics reveal how relationship addiction possesses the same self-destructive, insanity patterns of all addictions.

Must be love on the brain...that's got me feeling this way...beats me black and blue...but it (bleeps) me so good...and I can't get enough.

According to the F.B.I. crime report from 2011, over 10% of murders in the United States were committed by former lovers.

Like any addiction, not getting what you frantically desire can provoke feelings of rage even to the point of bloodshed. Of course, not everyone addicted to a relationship with someone becomes murderous at goodbye.

However, if you are addicted to someone, there are a host of other self-destructive, and even others-destructive, behaviors that you might exhibit.

According to Helen Fisher, a biological anthropologist at Rutgers University, "Nobody gets out of love alive. You turn into a menace or a pest when you've been rejected. That's when people stalk or commit suicide...there's a very powerful brain system (behind love addiction) that has a dramatic effect on your entire life."

The difference between
Love-*passion* and Love-*addiction*

Let's get bare-knuckle honest for a moment. All love relationships arouse within you a passionate desire for your object of affection; a slowly surging craving to have and hold the one you love. If you read *Song of Solomon* in the Old Testament, you will read phrases that express these passionate yearnings. For instance…

O my dove, in the clefts of the rock,
in the crannies of the cliff, let me see your face,
let me hear your voice,
for your voice is sweet,
and your face is lovely.
Catch the foxes for us,
the little foxes that
spoil the vineyards,
for our vineyards are in blossom."
My beloved is mine, and I am his;
he grazes among the lilies.
Until the day breathes and the shadows flee,
turn, my beloved, be like a gazelleor
a young stag on cleft mountains.

–Song of Solomon 2:14-17

But don't get it twisted—there is a definite difference between a Love-*passion* and a Love-*addiction*.

If you surmise you might have an addiction, consider the following symptoms offered by *Better Help*, the world's largest e-counseling platform. If you check off the majority of these symptoms, you may be addicted to your partner. I offer you the last symptom from my own research, one which best fits the subject of this book.

Alongside each of the symptoms, you will find a Bible verse that spells out what divine love looks like. This way, you are able to develop a contrast between dangerous love (addiction) and divine love (passion).

1. You lose self-control when triggered by your partner. *"Love is not easily provoked" (I Cor 13:5).*
2. You have no life outside the relationship. *"Love does not envy" (I Cor. 13:4).*
3. You endure a continual break-up and make-up cycle. *"Love is patient" (I Cor. 13:4).*
4. You rely upon sex for love. *"Love does not dishonor others. It is not self-seeking" (I Cor.13:5).*
5. You experience non-stop thinking about the relationship. *"Love always trusts" (I Cor. 13:6).*
6. You act in ways that contravene your beliefs, morals and ethics. *"Love does not delight in evil but rejoices in truth" (I Corinthians 13:6).*
7. You experience low self-esteem when triggered by your partner *"Love is kind" (I Corinthians 13:4).*
8. You are fully invested in a relationship that doesn't give you a satisfactory Return On Investment, a.k.a., R.O.I.

The Yokes

Oftentimes, your head tells you that you should leave, but your heart forbids you from doing so. The sensible part of you says, "Run!" but the sensual part of you says, "You ain't going nowhere!" Why can't you get away from this ASS?

Once again, employing farming terminology, you have become yoked to your partner. Somewhere along the way, your bond mutated into bondage. Let's take a closer look at specific kinds of yokes that will keep you stuck in a mismatched relationship longer than you know you should stay. Let's examine the yokes that hold OXEN hostage in an incompatible relationship with an ASS.

1. The Yoke of Chemicals

Studies by Burkett and Young (2012) reveal that mating and chemical addictions elicit the same neurochemical activity within the brain that involves a feel-good chemical known as dopamine. Both sex and chemical substances escalate levels of dopamine to a point where the participant experiences the same exact kind of rush. This study, along with many others, teach us that so-called love works just like any garden variety addiction.

No doubt, God designed our bodies to experience this chemical euphoria when we mate with the right person within a healthy context.

These feel-good sensations incentivize us to draw closer to our mates and forge an unbreakable bond between us that should last forever.

However, when these chemical sensations are released within a relationship that matches the criteria for a dangerous love, they become the yoke of an OX and an ASS.

Legendary artist Tina Turner was passionate about us not confusing these chemical sensations with true love in her song, "What's love got to do with it?"

The lyrics unmask the deception of chemicals as they often attempt to pose as love.

*You must understand…though the touch of your hand…makes my
pulse react…that it's only the thrill of boy meeting girl…*

The good news is, the brain can repair itself. Like any
addiction, according to researcher Helen Fisher, if you remain
abstinent for a period of time, studies have shown that the
cravings for your partner will wane as new neuropathways are
carved out within your brain. Idols are removed from the shelf
of your inner-self as you maintain a safe distance from them.

2. The Yoke of Control
In many cases, the reason why people don't leave a
relationship is because they have come under their partner's
control through years of being emotionally manipulated. In a
heathy union, one person *relates* to another; but in this kind of
relationship, one person *dominates* the other. In the movie, *The
Bronx Tale*, the mob boss Sony explains to Calogero that he
would rather be "feared than loved" because fear is a stronger
emotion. It is this motivating factor of fear that keeps many
OXEN stuck to ASS, yoked by means of control.

If you examine the interpersonal dynamics between Pharaoh
and the Hebrews in Exodus 5, you will observe how the yoke of
control works. First, Pharaoh *divides* the people by forbidding
them from congregating with each other and with their God
(Exodus 5:). Much like Pharaoh, often times, oppressive partners
will cut you off from your system of support, dividing you from
the very people who love you and protect you.

Second, Pharaoh *deprives* the people by taking away their
straw when transporting the bricks from Point A to Point B.
Given the fact that straw is what bundled the brick into one piece
after it came out of a hot furnace, depriving them of straw is

equivalent to withholding the stuff they needed to function. Controlling relationships deprive you of the stuff you need to function—money, sex, affection, praise, safety, etc. The theory of negative reinforcement teaches us that this would actually motivate people to stay out of fear of what else might be taken away. The Hebrews probably reasoned, "He took my straw away! If I try leaving, what else will he take away!"

Third, Pharaoh *demeans* the people by calling them names—"Lazy!" Pharaoh hollers. A demeaning name plays on our psyche, and has the power to shape how we see ourselves. Inside of a tattoo shop in Hong Kong, a man strangely had the phrase, "Loser" branded on his flesh. An onlooker asked the Chinese Tattoo artist, "How could someone in their right mind do such a thing?" The sagacious tattoo artist replied, "Before tattoo on body, tattoo on mind."

You've reached the apex of a controlling relationship when your oppressor's words fuse into your every thought.

After years of being divided, deprived and demeaned, the Hebrews came under Pharaoh's yoke of control; the same kind of yoke that keeps an OX joined to an ASS.

3. The Yoke of Convenience

According to Dr. Lurve, Australia's leading expert in the subject of relationships, all of the inconveniences caused by a breakup serve as a negative reinforcement that keeps people yoked together. Questions such as, "How will I financially survive without my partner? Who will help me raise my kids? What will happen with our home?" play the most pivotal role in keeping people together, even in the most toxic situations. The more you have become reliant upon your partner, the more likely you are to remain within that relationship.

**Faithful and stuck often look alike;
many people who appear to be faithful are really
just stuck with no other options.**

In Exodus 16, after being emancipated from the harsh conditions of Egypt, the Hebrews actually gaze back at their captivity with longing! They express their desire to return to the very situation from which they experienced a dramatic deliverance. Notice in Exodus 16:3, the particular feature that allures them to revert back to such an oppressive circumstance. The Hebrews bellow, "There we sat around pots of meat and ate all of the food we wanted." In other words, "There, life was more convenient for us." It was the yoke of convenience that joined the souls of the Hebrews to the Egyptians.

4. The Yoke of Co-dependency
Lastly, the yoke of co-dependency holds many people hostage in a relationship that's depleting them rather than completing them. This yoke is especially common when mating with someone who has some kind of ailment such as addiction or mental/physical illness.

According to Melody Beattie in her book, *Co-dependent No More*, co-dependency can be simply defined as "the loss of oneself." This means that you have become so fixated with fixing your partner that you have lost your own self. When you have come under the yoke of co-dependency, you lose touch with your own preferences, principles and promises. It becomes all about helping, fixing or changing the other person to a point where your own personhood does not exist anymore. Therefore, the utter emptiness that would follow the end of your relationship with that person is too unbearable. You stay because you would have nothing of yourself left to return to, given the fact that you invested everything you had in helping your partner.

Sneak-peak of what's ahead

Chances are, you've identified a few keys by reading the last couple of chapters. First, you determined whether you are an OX mating with an ASS. Second, you figured out whether you are addicted to your partner. Third, you discerned the nature of the yoke(s) that keep you stuck in that relationship.

All of this begs the question, "How do I break the yokes that bind me?"

From a farming perspective, only the master can remove the yoke from the neck of two animals.

Likewise, nothing short of divine intervention will enable you to sever such a deeply spiritual, emotional and neurological bond with someone.

Nonetheless, there are some practical measures you can take in participating in your own liberation. God will not supernaturally deliver those who make no efforts towards freedom with the means He has naturally granted them. It is incumbent upon you to take some steps towards freedom. You must get moving! God will deliver you from any pit you fall into, but He will not deliver you from your armchair. The following chapters offer a series of steps in breaking free from dangerous yokes based on research, biblical references and the stories of people who have made a successful exodus from toxic situations.

CHAPTER THREE
Eat Healthy

"Do not muzzle the ox when it is treading out the grain"(Deuteronomy 25:4).

DON'T MUZZLE THE OX

The Bible highlights this ancient law in Deuteronomy to remind us of the vital significance of permitting an animal to eat,especially when its expending energy. If the farmer expects a productive animal, it behooves him to allow his animal to partake from the ground while performing its duties. A good farmer knows that working without eating will cause a breakdown.

Pay attention all you OXEN—performing without partaking is a sure recipe for burnout!

If you are an OX, you are predisposed to *give* of yourself more than you *get* for yourself. You are likely to run yourself ragged for others while taking no time to nurture yourself. In doing so, you are muzzling your mind from the nutrition required to function. If a farmer muzzles his ox, the animal will eventually lose its stamina, and collapse under the heat of the sun from endless giving without any regular getting. In the same manner, if you muzzle your mind, you will soon crackup from a deficiency of spiritual strength.

I knew I was burnt out from my own involvement with toxic-relationships when I found myself fantasizing about how relaxing jail would be. Of course, I say this comically, but I knew I was depleted when I found myself visiting a friend at a mental hospital and inquiring, "How long do they let you stay in this place? What do you have to say to the doctors for them to commit you?"

All kidding aside, the burnout that comes from being muzzled—the performing without partaking—makes you desperately want to check out of your circumstances.

If you are psychologically falling apart, could the basis of your breakdown have something to do with a lack of nutrition? If you are the kind of person who sacrifices time and energy for people, but hardly ever nourishes yourself, a collapse of some sort is inevitable. Every muzzled mind is on its way towards a personal crisis.

**Psychological breakdowns happen when
you spend lots of time with people who NEED you
but little time with people who FEED you.**

Meditation

The spiritual nourishment of your mind is critical, not merely for breaking free from toxic-relationships, but for your overall existence. Just as your body requires food and water to survive, your mind yearns for truth to stay alive.

Interestingly enough, the Greek term used in the Bible for meditate can be defined as "chewing on the cud"—the act of an animal regurgitating its food in order to glean the most nutrients from its sustenance.

Spiritual nourishment can be defined as meditating, or chewing, on spiritual truths repeatedly and regularly.

Perhaps you're thinking, "I don't know how to meditate!"

Let me ask you this question—do you know how to worry?

For instance, do you worry about your partner relapsing?

Do you worry about returning home after work, unsure of what mood they will be in?

Do you worry about your partner leaving you?

Now think about what your mind does when you worry. You repeatedly mull on the same thought over and over again. You obsessively rehash all of the *"What if?"* scenarios that relate to your circumstances.

It's the same motion the mind makes when meditating. If you know how to worry, then you know how to meditate.

Make no mistake about it, meditation is *instinctual*; however, what we choose to meditate upon is *intentional*. If we meditate upon fearful possibilities, we get tired. But if we meditate upon spiritual principles, we get inspired. In order to grow in virtues like courage and clarity—the stuff needed to come out of an unhealthy relationship—set time aside every day to meditate upon spiritual truths even if it's only ten minutes in the morning before you leave for work.

A supervisory heart
with a submissive head

If you are an OX, chances are you have a supervisory heart (emotions) with a submissive head (cognitions). If you are an OX, your heart calls the shots while your head just goes along. When it's time to make a decision, your heart commands while your head buries itself in the sand. If you are an OX, your feelings are forever overriding facts. For instance...

- *Facts* are, my partner keeps getting high. But my *feelings* say, if I love him/her a little more, I can change them.

- *Facts* are, my partner keeps physically hurting me. But my *feelings* say, If I didn't bother him/her, they wouldn't hurt me.
- *Facts* are, my partner keeps cheating on me. But my *feelings* say, If I lose weight, they won't look for someone else.
- *Facts* are, my partner makes me feel very unworthy and unlovely. But my *feelings* say, I can't live without them.

When you are an OX with a submissive head and a supervisory heart, your feelings are forever outweighing the facts. When you are an OX with a passive head but an overactive heart, you acquiesce to what you feel even at the expense of your discernment of what's real. Music sensation Ariana Grande captures the delusional mindset of an OX when involved with an ASS in her song, "In My Head."

Painted a picture…I thought I knew you well…I got a habit of seeing what isn't there

With this kind of makeup, you are easily taken advantage of by less sensitive types. Having a heart with so many strings makes you susceptible to being jerked around in all sorts of directions. Think about how many times your partner pulled your heartstrings this week alone, manipulating you into doing whatever they wished you to do. By pulling the string of fear, perhaps threatening you with "Divorce" or maybe shaming you in front of your friends, your partner intimidates you into obedience. By yanking the string of guilt, maybe telling you how you fall short of your wifely or husbandly duties, your partner manipulates you into compliance.

Feeding your head

News alert! If your heart rules your head, this is not the way that God designed you to function. Your Maker fashioned your mind so that your prefrontal cortex (the center of your reasoning) regulates your amygdala (the hub of your emotions). For instance, your amygdala signals your prefrontal cortex with a feeling of fear. When this happens, it is the role of your prefrontal cortex to justify or dismiss that fear. In some cases, such as a car heading towards you at 50 mph, your prefrontal cortex justifies the fear and prompts you to swift action. In other cases, such as being threatened with abandonment that will lead to a lifetime of loneliness, your prefrontal cortex dismisses that fear as sensational hype. Your Maker designed you in such a way that your head brings clarity and guidance to your heart.

If you expect your head to assume its rightful place over your heart, then you must feed your head to become stronger than your heart. Notice in Philippians 4, when the Apostle Paul offers a remedy for anxiety, he states, "*Think* on these things (the truths of God's Word)." The Apostle Paul does not make his appeal to the heart by saying, "*Feel* these things" instead, he petitions our heads to "*Think* these things." What's suggested is that we can think our way into right feeling, but we cannot feel our way into right thinking.

**Feed your head so that it is
strong enough to rule your heart.**

Our Survey: The real-life people we spoke to who escaped toxic-relationships.

Remo   Meg   Ani

Stan   Vilma   Paul

A heartfelt thanks to the guys and gals who were willing to share their stories with me after breaking free from toxic-relationships.

Names have been changed for the sake of privacy.

I complied all the data I collected during these surveys and documented it under "SURVEY SAYS…" at the end of each of the following chapters in this book.

You will discover the particular truths from the Bible and other inspired literature and media that strengthened the minds of these guys and gals for their great escape.

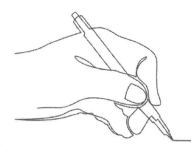

Notes from our "Eat Healthy" survey:
Here's what those who LEFT the relationship said:

Ani, a brave young woman who made her exodus after weathering five years of an ASS's addiction and abuse, meditated upon Isaiah 43:2, 18-19 and 54:2-27. *Ani* recommends, *"The Christian Codependence Recovery Workbook: From Surviving to Significance"* by Stephanie A. Tucker, a book that exposed faulty self-concepts that kept her locked up within her dungeon. *Ani* suggests, *"I Am: a 60-Day Journey To Knowing Who You are Because of Who He Is"*, by Michele Cushatt, a book that empowered her to withstand emotional manipulation by placing her confidence in Christ.

Meg, a lady who endured decades of selfishness that included extra-marital affairs, focused on verses in the Bible that elevated her standards for picking a godly man. Being far too easily pleased, it did her well to raise her sights by reading I Timothy 6:11. Also, she reflected on Proverbs 31 so that she could become the quality of woman that would find favor with God.

Stan, a middle-aged man who sacrificed eighteen years of his life to a relationship that ended with addiction and adultery, claims it was the book of Proverbs that gave him much needed wisdom to navigate hostile situations. *Stan* says it was the literature from his Al Anon group that helped him break the yoke of co-dependency; adages such as "If it's not yours, don't pick it up" and "The Three C's: I didn't Cause it, I can't Cure it and I can't Control it" became trends of thought that helped him take his life back. *Stan* claims it was a sermon by Bishop T.D. Jakes called, 'The Blame Game" that settled his anger, satiated his need to get even, and enabled him to focus on solutions rather than situations.

Remo, a devout churchman and family-man, finally bolted after eighteen years of emotional abandonment, adulterous affairs and abuse. He says, "Dr. Myles Monroe's *Divorce, Remarriage and Singleness* was a real game-changer in my old-school thinking on these topics. I was probably more bound by my staunch ideas than I was by the circumstances. Dr. Monroe set me free from that narrow lens."

Here's what those who STAYED in the relationship yet broke free from the toxic dynamics said:

Vilma Says, "When I became aware of my husband's addiction to pornography and relapse on drugs I was initially devastated. The betrayal, lies, and secrecy broke any trust I had in him and the pain caused me to push him away. I remember thinking 'How could he do this to me and our children?' At that point, I began reading literature about the addictive grip of pornography and books about the healing of the heart once trust is broken. One of the greatest takeaways of all that reading was a wife who shared so honestly about how selfish her love was towards husband. She shared how not once during the revelation of his 'shameful secret' did she consider 'how is my husband's soul?'

But instead she was consumed with how he had hurt her. I began to see how selfish my love was as well and asked the Lord to change my heart to look more like his. I realized that I could learn to let the Lord heal my heart and that it wasn't dependent on his behavior. I also realized that his behavior had very little if nothing to do with me. Learning to come alongside him in the battle for his soul became my mission."

Paul says, "As long as I've been a born-again Christian, I've always relentlessly pursued to bridge the divide between the flesh and the spirit man. The Holy Spirit has recently let me to see that this bridge that I have tried to create has already been created by God in the soul of man. The scripture about loving the Lord your God with ALL of my heart, soul, mind and strength reveals four very distinct parts meant to work in conjunction with one another. This passage along with some books on soul health has brought me to a place of being whole so that I can in turn, love wholly. I lived so fragmented that essentially I was giving and loving the Lord and others with 100% of only 50% of myself. As the Spirit has led me into truth and dismantled lies, He has pieced me back together to live fully."

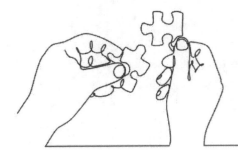

Putting the pieces together: The "Eat Healthy" Challenge.

- Meditate upon one of the recommended Bible passages, along with your own preferred passages, for fifteen minutes every morning and fifteen minutes every night for ninety days.
- Read three of the recommended books or authors from the survey notes within the next ninety days.
- Consult one or more of any recommended book or media clip for the next ninety days.
- Keep a journal, logging your "Truth-Nutrients" as you engage in the eating habits suggested in the previous chapter.

CHAPTER FOUR
Carry Your Load

"For each one should carry his own load" (Galatians 6:6).

YOU'RE ONLY KEEPING YOURSELF WARM

Setting aside the fact that you're an OX, a selfless, generous person, you're more than likely getting something out of the relationship with this ASS. Without some incentive, you would have no motivation to stay.

Granted, the reward is probably far less than what you truly deserve and maybe consisting of more empty promises than fulfilled wishes. But, be not deceived in assuming that there isn't some carrot dangling in purview to keep you hoping.

Perhaps you're offended by me suggesting that you're getting something out of this ordeal with such a deadbeat. Maybe it touches a nerve for me to insinuate that you receive some form of compensation for the sacrifices you make. We all like to see ourselves as selfless martyrs motivated by pure love. Nonetheless, such pure altruism does not exist unless you were born of a virgin by way of immaculate conception (sarcasm). Under the light of truth, you will be surprised to find out that your greatest acts of kindness are motivated by some self-serving purpose.

Let me break it down for you like this:

Two ladies walk by a pet store window on a frigid December evening. Within the store window, they spot two puppies cuddling up with one another.

The first lady naïvely says, "Look how wonderful! They are keeping each other warm!"

The second wiser lady says, "Wrong. They are keeping themselves warm." To the indiscriminate eye, our *giving*

60

masquerades our *getting*. But from God's fully discerning perspective, even our most noble deeds are assessed as "filthy rags" (Isaiah 64:6).

Could it be that you're keeping yourself warm just as much as you are keeping your partner warm?

As draining as your relationship might be, face the fact that you are getting something out of this deal.

Different types of incentives

If you plan on making an exodus from this toxic-relationship, it would serve you well to identify your incentives.

Do yourself a favor by abandoning this idea of yourself as Mother Theresa or Gandhi or some other martyr who loves without any strings attached. Instead, come to terms with the fact that you are being baited by something to stay in such a crazy situation.

Why is it so important to identify the incentives? Because when you identify the thing that baits you, you have also figured out the thing that binds you.

By recognizing the thing that entices you, you have also realized the thing that enslaves you.

**Whatever entices you has the
power to enslave you.**

On the next page, you will find a list of possible incentives that keep you committed to this relationship. There's a good chance that these enticements are never truly obtained but merely waved in front of you like that a carrot before the rabbit.

1. My partner is my PAL. For some, the reality of being alone is so unbearable that just the idea of having someone at home is an incentive to stay in this relationship. According to research, forty percent of women surveyed claimed that they were afraid of being alone while thirty-five percent of men admitted the same dread. Monophobia, the fear of being by your lonesome, is kept at bay by staying with your partner.

2. My partner is my PROVIDER. For others, keeping the wolf from the door seems impossible without the financial assistance of their partners. In a study conducted by One Poll, involving 2,000 married and cohabitating women, over two-thirds of the respondents depending upon their partner as provider felt trapped in the relationship. In a study conducted by Barber in 2003, it was found that women were more likely to divorce if they had their own economic means.

3. My partner is my LOVER. Obviously not in all cases, but in some situations, spicy sex holds a person hostage in a bad relationship. In 2016, Canadian scientists carried out research on how sex strips people of common sense, creating a "tunnel vision" in which the only focus is alleviating erotic tension. In the words of the late Robin Williams, "God made one mistake when he made the male body. He created a penis and a brain but not enough blood to operate both at the same time." In other words, it is impossible to be horny and intelligent simultaneously.

4. My Partner is my SCAPEGOAT. Strangely, your partner plays a wonderful scapegoat; an object to blame for whatever goes wrong in life. Granted, in many cases, your partner may be eligible for much blame. However, it still serves you to have them around to deflect from your own defects; as long as you stay with your partner, you are too distracted by their issues to work on your issues. Scapegoats are objects of blame that conveniently divert your attention from feeling your own personal shame. In the words of the gangster Tony Montana in the movie, *Scarface*, "You need people like me so you can't point your finger (away from yourself) and say, 'That's the bad guy.'"

5. My partner is my SERVANT. Whether it be taxi-driving the kids, keeping the house clean, doing the laundry or fixing broken appliances, many people rely upon their partner to hold the fort down. Leaving your partner flies in the face of your desire for an easy life.

Carry your load

Galatians 6:6 states, "For each one should carry his own load." In the original Greek language, the term "load" is defined as "tasks and roles that belong to you personally, nontransferable to another person."

For instance, you are responsible for your own thinking, believing, speaking or choosing; these functions are all classified as non-transferable loads along with a list of others. Any relationship where you rely upon your partner to think, believe, speak or choose for you, or vice versa, is a co-dependent bond that must be broken.

More often than not, partnering with someone who carries your "load" comes with an expense. He/she might make all the decisions for you, but what's it costing you? He/she might do all your bidding for you, but what's the fee? I have a friend who refuses to ask for money from her husband. When I inquired why, she said, "I never ask for money in order to avoid hearing his opposing opinion. If I don't take the money, I don't have to deal with the opinion." In this scenario, if she took any money from him, she would inadvertently forfeit her right to choose.

When Galatians 6:6 advises you to carry our own load, it is implicitly telling you to establish independence. You might mate with someone who performs culinary magic in the kitchen for you, or repairs your broken car engine, but neither of these kind gestures should cost you your autonomy. God gave you two feet so that you could stand up on your own!

In what ways have you become reliant upon your partner for the wrong things? Or, what are you losing in the process of this relationship? It is time to establish some independence, a.k.a. carry your own load, so that you are no longer trapped in this relationship. Take into account the ways that our OXEN learned to carry their own loads, hence making them less dependent upon their ASSES.

Notes from our "Carrying Your Load" survey:
Here's what those who LEFT the relationship said:

Stan became reliant upon his wife's opinion for everything. The bond with his wife was like the relationship between a ventriloquist and his puppet. Stan had no voice of his own, but merely echoed her feelings and thoughts. He was so lost in her that he only liked what she liked, believed what she believed and chose what she chose. Not suddenly but subtly, Stan learned to stand on his two feet. Little by little, Stan carried his own load in this area by engaging in certain activities by himself. For instance, he frequented the movies by himself when his wife worked rather than staying home waiting for her arrival. At the movie theater, he selected the movie he wanted to see, ordered the candy he liked and sat in the row he preferred. This may sound silly for some, but these were strides towards freedom for Stan.

Meg says she relied upon her partner as a nanny or a shoddy version of Mr. Belvedere while she went to work fulltime to take care of the household expenses that come with raising a child. She didn't care for his character, or even his personality, so the relationship was purely convenient. Over the course of time, Meg worked diligently at developing her own relationship with her daughter that didn't require his assistance. Also, she learned to balance the demands of her profession with household chores so that she wouldn't need her butler's sloppy services. These steps weaned her from the need of the ASS in carrying these loads.

Remo says, "I wanted her to want me. The more she deprived me of sex, the more I starved for her approval and affection. Man, she used sex like hypnosis! Plus, I didn't want to be embarrassed in the public eye by leaving her. I held public offices and knew the divorce might spark controversy. For me, weaning meant drawing that affection from other wellsprings—Jesus, friends and my daughters. My daughters especially. Carrying my load meant carrying their load and being a road-map for them."

Ani says, "We were together since we were twenty years old. I invested so much time in our relationship. I invested so much time in helping him. I was the only one who could calm him down when he lost his temper. I held him together, and that felt good. I guess I needed to be needed by him. The weaning happened by just getting tired of playing that role. After lying in a hospital bed with a broken collar bone from being smashed to the ground by him in a drunken fit. Oh, and worrying about my daughter being put in danger from his drug activities. From all that, I was weaned. I learned to carry my own load by virtue of survival. In addition, I think that his craziness helped deflect my attention from my own insecurities. In that regard, carrying my own load meant coming to terms with my own imperfections without feeling condemned. I didn't need him as a scapegoat anymore when I could do that."

Here's what those who STAYED the relationship but broke free from toxic dynamics said:

Vilma says, "In the beginning of our marriage, I relied on my husband's mood to indicate whether or not I was doing a good enough job as a wife, mother, worker, and housekeeper. When he was irritated or criticized me I would 'work harder' to make him happy. I grew to resent him. I also held the expectation that he needed to communicate with me in the ways that I thought were best. If he would not or could not resolve a conflict with me I lost all sense of peace; therefore, the status of our unity deeply affected my sense of well-being. I began to see that our individual wounding was deeply affecting both of our abilities to effectively communicate and resolve conflict. The Lord began to humble both of us in some profound ways and after walking through truly forgiving him I began to learn to accept him as he was and not demand he change. I began to learn to rely on how the Lord saw me and cultivated a mindset of knowing He approved of me. This became my foundation when my husband's moods would fluctuate. It was finding my worth and acceptance in Jesus that set me free from the bondage of relying on my spouse in an unhealthy way."

Paul says, "I relied on my wife in an unhealthy manner by seeking respect and validation from her because I was wounded and lacked self-respect from my past relationships and some traumas I have received. This brokenness in me necessitated her to fill a void that she was never designed to fill. And I actually penalized her in many ways for not meeting this void. This created a deeper void and a consistent disconnect between us and myself and the Lord. Only when I began to allow the Holy Spirit to uncover, dig out and heal some roots and broken belief systems did I begin to feast on the truth of who I really am. This fed my soul in a healthy way that caused me to abide in the love of God in such a way that my cravings for my wife's respect now became fueled by a selfless perspective not on what she could give me but on what I already had in Christ. This new identification became a platform to actually see and love her, even in her brokenness, which created a healthy cycle of care and nurturing that was not self-driven but Spirit-led."

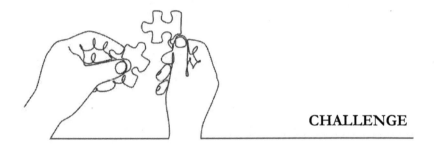

CHALLENGE

Putting the pieces together: "The Carry Your Load" Challenge

- Identify the list of incentives that keep you stuck in toxic relationship dynamics.
- Talk over with your therapist, pastor or trusted friend these incentives and how to break free from such a yoke.
- Learn to carry your own load within these areas. Make strides towards independence, learning to stand on your own feet.
- Anticipate a weaning process whereby you experience withdrawal-symptoms by not looking to your partner anymore in that area.

CHAPTER FIVE

Use Your Horns

*"God brings them out of Egypt. He is for them like
the horns of the wild ox" (Numbers 23:22).*

USE YOUR HORNS

Fortunately, the OX is not some defenseless creature, tossed into the wilderness at the mercy of besieging wildlife. On the contrary, the OX was created by God with a protective mechanism known as horns. These God-given, pointy-tipped, spiral-shaped projections are used to enforce distance between the OX and its fellow species, guarding whatever territory belongs to that animal. Just the sight of the horns alone makes a bold statement to all surrounding wildlife: "Stand back!"

Now of course, some animals are more intrusive than others, being defiant rather than compliant to the OX's horns. But these animals learn the hard way that the OX is not an animal to be trifled with.

You too have horns!

As helpless as you may feel, you possess the God-given, inalienable right to enforce boundaries with the ASSES in your life.

You have the prerogative to say, "No!" when you don't want to do something.

You have the right to say, 'Stand Back!" when you need space from him or her.

You have the authority to say, "Back up or else!" when your wishes aren't being respected.

And you have the entitlement to follow through with whatever consequences are warranted when your wishes aren't respected—a phone-call to the police, reaching out to your lawyer, an act of physical self-defense, etc. Pity the person who misconstrues your kindness for weakness.

Like the OX, you might be sweet, but you are not a person to be toyed with!

An easy-mark

Over the last several decades, the F.B.I. interviewed countless sexual predators inquiring about the characteristics they sought after in a victim. One of the most typical scenarios that sexual predators described to F.B.I. agents was approaching a young lady on a sidewalk or in a parking lot. As the predator came within her reach, the first gesture was to offer her a piece of gum. If she declined, the predator would offer again. If the lady barked back in any way, the predator bolted from her company. But if she accepted the gum, she showed herself to be the type of person who *Goes Along to Get Along*. Sexual predators specifically target those who emit the scent of passivity while forgoing those who have horns.

Going Along to Get Along is what makes you appear to be an Easy-Mark to the wildlife of our society.

Let me land this plane where you live. You go along to get along with sexual games that make you feel grimy. You go along to get along with squandering money you deem as unwise. You go along to get along with befriending people you discern as untrustworthy. You go along to get along with ideas that seem irresponsible at best, and reckless at worse. You go along to get along with accepting realities that fly in the face of your ideals. You go along to get along—even retreating from your relationship with the people you love, maybe even God! Let's face the facts—you have the appearance of being an *Easy-Mark* with idle horns.

The following story, featured in my previous book *Pen Your Pain Into Parables*, I wrote about my own lifelong struggle with being an *Easy-Mark*. Perhaps you can identify with my people-pleasing tendency and the cost that comes with this issue.

Don't pick up what's not yours

"Michael, hold this for one second please," my buddy insists while handing over his Snickers. "Sure thing," I respond accommodatingly.

Examining the candy-bar a bit closer, I detect there's nothing left of the delicacy but a caramel-stained wrapper. Further away into the school yard, just beyond the trash barrel, I spot my buddy chuckling with the other tots looking back at me. It's one of those typical fourth grade games where the kids pick on the buffoon of the bunch. This is not the first time he hoodwinked me into taking ownership of his trash. I'm always an easy-mark, because I am the simpleton who *Goes Along to Get Along*.

Moseying towards the trash barrel to discard the plastic wrapper, I hear the school-bell chime and the kids sprint back towards class. Twenty minutes before recess began, Mrs. Fields announced that the tot who arrives back the earliest gets the opportunity to select this afternoon's storybook. I would outrun everyone back to class so we could listen to Mrs. Fields mimic Aslan's doting voice while reciting "The Lion, the Witch and the Wardrobe." But when the school bell chimed, I am strolling south towards the trash barrel while my classmates dash north towards the prize. This was a habit that would haunt me for years to follow; I forego wonderful opportunities for myself because I am too preoccupied with taking out another's trash.

Returning to class about forty seconds later than everyone else, I hear Mrs. Fields reading a book by Judy Bloom; a tale I consider puddle-deep in comparison to the intellectual profundity of CS Lewis. "Shucks! I missed my chance!" I fume. My buddy pivots his head towards me and impishly grins while listening to the storybook of his selection.

Resentment bubbles up within me like a shaken soda-bottle just before opening the cap.

I think about how many times I've been beaten because I *Go along to get along*. It would take another several decades for me to realize a truth that would spare me a great deal of unnecessary grief. If it's not yours, don't pick it up.

The relationship between insecurity and a lack of boundaries

Perhaps you're pondering, "Why do I have such a tough time enforcing boundaries?"

The short answer to this question is the term, insecurity. Consider the etymology of the term, insecurity: the term, *in,* means "without" whereas the term, *security* means "boundaries." It stands to reason that the telltale sign of insecurity is having a lack of boundaries.

True to its operational definition, insecurity means to lack confidence in your own worth. Wherever there be a lack of worth, there be also a lack of boundaries. For instance, you probably won't find any security systems around junkyards. On the other hand, you will find security system inside and outside of banks. Why? Boundaries are only enforced where worth is realized. When you realize your worth, you will inevitably utilize your horns to protect yourself. You will use your horns more naturally when you have an epiphany of your worth.

Your Pearls

In any toxic-relationship, one or more of the following areas will beckon for the usage of your horns. Let's call these areas the *valuables* of your life that deserve your protection. These are your *pearls*—the riches of your life that should never *be tossed to the swine only to be trampled underfoot* (Matthew 7:6). Chances are, the ASSES in your life have infringed upon one or more of the following areas; a clear sign that it is time to use your horns. Alongside each pearl, you will find a correlating bible verse.

- Your Trust (Matthew 7:16)
- Your Time (Ephesians 5:16)
- Your Thoughts and Feelings (Proverbs 4:23)
- Your Sexuality (I Corinthians 6:19-20)
- Your Purpose (Romans 8:30-31)
- Your Relationship with God (I John 3:7)
- Your Relationship with Others (Philippians 2:3)
- Your Morals and Values (Psalm 1:1)
- Your Possessions (Proverbs 3:9)
- Your Name (Proverbs 22:1)

Suggestions on enforcing boundaries

For OXEN who naturally serve others without regard for their own limitations, enforcing boundaries is not an easy task. Below, you will find some wisdom from modern psychology as well as the timeless Bible on enforcing boundaries with the ASSES in your life.

1.   Identify the Pearls of Your Life (Matthew 7:6).

Once again, you have to recognize your worth in order to become more instinctual about using your horns. Boundaries are only enforced where worth is recognized.

2.   Tune Into Your Spirit (I Corinthians 14:33)

When you feel uneasy, confused or troubled by what was said or done by someone, listen to the signals of your spirit. Take some space from that person in order to discern if a boundary has been violated. Confusion or uneasiness is often a sign that a boundary has been crossed.

3.   Determine the Boundary Lines (Psalm 16:6)

Take some time to determine where the boundary lines must be established. For instance, you might be okay with talking on the phone with someone but decide not to meet with them in person. It needs to be clear to you before you can make it clear to someone else. A cloud over your reasoning will translate to a heavy fog over their minds.

4.   Determine the Consequences (Matthew 18:17)

You must determine the recourse that needs to be taken if the ASSES do not listen and/or respect your boundaries. Chance are, there will be a backlash of some sort to your stance. Just because you are done with them abusing you doesn't mean that they are done abusing you.

5.   Say What You Mean (Matthew 5:33)

Do not pussyfoot around saying what needs to be said. Get right to the point with clear, concise speech that accurately presents the line you're drawing in the sand. When you pussyfoot, or speak in vague generalities, you give off the impression that you're afraid. And predators, as well as controlling people, are empowered by fear!

6. Mean What You Say (Matthew 5:37)

After all is said and done, may there not be more said than done! Your words only become credible as you back them up with action. Conversely, you lose all authority when you establish boundaries you aren't willing to enforce.

7. Don't Say It Mean (Ephesians 4:15)

You don't need to be cruel to be tough. You can make your point known clearly and directly in a spirit of love.

8. Don't Pick Up What's Not Yours (Proverbs 4:23)

Do not let yourself be intimidated, guilt-tripped or manipulated as you are enforcing your boundaries. You will probably have to withstand all of these tactics from the ASSES in your life. These are tactics geared towards getting you to assume more responsibility than what truly belongs to you.

9. Assume His Yoke Alone (Matthew 11:30)

Keep your plan simple by only doing what Jesus wants you to do. Focus exclusively on doing the next right thing He places in front of you. When we serve in this manner, we live under an easy yoke with far less stress. More will be mentioned about this subject in the chapters that follow.

10. Yoke with Other OXEN (Proverbs 27:17)

You will need the support and accountability of other OXEN to enforce your boundaries. More will be mentioned about this subject in the chapters that follow.

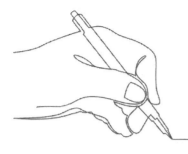

SURVEY SAYS...

Notes from our 'Use Your Horns' survey:

Here's what those who LEFT the relationship:

Ani, the lady who looped all four A-Circles, states that she established the following boundaries after reaching her breaking point. First, she insisted that her ex-husband leave the home. Second, she hid from him until she was resilient enough to see him, but only to discuss their child. Third, she met him face to face in a safe place with a letter explicitly stating her boundaries. She left him with a letter so that he could revisit the boundaries she laid out. Fourth, she blocked him from her phone for a designated window of time after any incident of verbal abuse. Lastly, she relied upon third parties to mediate whenever necessary.

Stan, a man whose wife plunged into addiction and adultery, says that he had to leave the house for his own sanity. He claims that he could not heal in the same environment in which he was damaged. Even if it meant sleeping on his relative's couch, he resolved to value his own peace more than comfort.

Meg avows that her greatest boundary was her ignore-muscle, the ability to forgo on every trap that came her way. She says, "I finally decided to stop participating. I finally resolved that he would no longer rope me into senseless feuds. I decided that I didn't have to attend every argument I was invited to. I was my boundary. I was the keeper of my peace"

Remo says, "Man, I gotta be honest. I had no boundaries. I just submitted to whatever demand she put on me even through the divorce. My warped sense of worth made me think that I had no right to object. I wish I could take some credit for breaking free from that long relationship, but it was all God using some the circumstances to pave my way out."

Here's what those who STAYED within the relationship but broke free from toxic dynamics said:

Vilma says, "When I realized the extent to which my husband struggled with pornography and a need to be noticed by other women, we enforced quite a few boundaries for his protection as well as for our marriage. He agreed to them and didn't push back. Some of those boundaries were restrictions on his phone, my ability to check his phone, location services activated, and a change in his occupation which didn't leave him with unoccupied amounts of time."

Paul says, "The one boundary that I needed to enforce was mostly on myself. I needed to give myself the space to process with Jesus before I reacted to a situation. Also, this boundary kept me from passive aggressively looking outward without looking inward first."

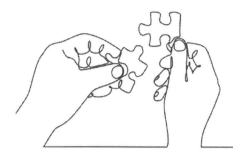

Putting the pieces together: The 'Use Your Horns' Challenge

- List your pearls in a journal.
- Determine your boundaries as well as the ensuing consequences for crossing them.
- Seek counsel from a trusted person on relaying those boundaries to the ASS in your life.
- Practice using your horns with a trusted person by role-playing.
- Ask a trusted person to hold you accountable to the boundaries you lay out.

CHAPTER SIX
Stay Close to The Herd

"Two are better than one, because they have a good return for their labor. If either of them falls down, one can help the other up. But pity anyone who falls and has no one to help them up" (Ecclesiastes 4:9–4:10).

THE HERD

Oxen are known to voyage seventy deep in one single herd in order to protect each other from the predators of the wild. When under threat, they "circle the wagon" which means they form a circle with their horns pointing forward while their vulnerable populations remain in the middle. Without help from the herd, vulnerable populations—such as those who are small, sickly or just stupid—are at risk of being devoured by predacious beasts.

Oxen know the golden rule of survival in the wild: Stay close to the herd!

If you've been stuck in a toxic-relationship for an extended period of time, you are far more vulnerable than you even realize. Studies in behavioral science have shown the hazardous effects of a toxic-relationship on health. For instance, one study that tracked 10,000 participants stranded in a negative relationship for over twelve years showed a higher likelihood of heart disease and even cardiac arrest amongst its participants. Other studies have shown that prolonged exposure to contentious situations result in the same damage done to the brain as being in war.

Well, that should be no surprise since the realities of a toxic-relationship resemble the jungles of Vietnam—always looking over your shoulder, living under the threat of what's coming, guarded all the time, and feeling fatigued from the ongoing struggle.

Given the fact that you are a vulnerable person surrounded by wildlife, you too need a herd. The mentioned data underscores the importance of staying close to your herd in order to remain safe in a dangerous world. So then, who is your herd? Sadly, the qualifications for a trusted relationship have diluted in our shallow society to including someone who makes you laugh, shows you a good-time and nods "Yes" to every decision you make. Trusted relationships, a.k.a "your herd" are so much more than tickling your funny bone or stroking your ego. A good herd will provide you with the following FOUR BENEFITS, all of which we will discuss at greater length in the following sections of this chapter.

These benefits are laid out in Ecclesiastes 4:9-12, a portion of scripture that identifies the assets that come from a trusted relationship.

1. Accountability: *"Two are better than one, because they have a good return for their labor" (Ecclesiastes 4:9).*

2. Advocacy: *"If either of them falls down, one can help the other up. But pity anyone who falls and has no one to help them up" (Ecclesiastes 4:10).*

3. Comradery: *If two lie down together, they will keep warm. But how can one can warm alone" (Ecclesiastes 4:11).*

4. Safety: *Though one may be overpowered, two can defend themselves" (Ecclesiastes 4:12).*

Accountability

Far too often, in our endeavor to break free from toxic-relationships, we make assertions without following through with action. We vow to speak up for ourselves. Yet, the fear of some kind of backlash from our partner delays our duties. We pledge to enforce a particular boundary. Yet, a feeling of hopelessness, a thought such as *"It won't work"*, impedes our movement. We swear to ourselves "I'm leaving the ASS by this time next week." Yet, the fear of being alone cancels our plans. And, after all is said and done, there is usually more *said* than *done*.

The beauty of joining a herd is that it raises the likelihood of our assertions translating to actions. According to Solomon, by partnering up with the right people, we produce a better "return for our labor." In other words, we actually produce what we promised. Because of the right partnerships, we actually walk out what we talk about.

Perhaps the main reason we become more action-oriented is because of something called *accountability*. Having a herd equates to having one or more individuals who hold you to your word. According to business mogul Bob Proctor, "accountability is the glue that ties commitment to the result." The herd will ask you questions such as:

"Did you sit down with your partner?"

"How did it go with telling them how you feel?"

"Have you maintained that boundary?"

"Did you find a new job so that you no longer rely on your partner financially?"

These are the questions that fasten our assertions to actions, or the glue that binds our commitments to the results.

Your herd might come in the form of a church family, a support group, a clinical therapist, a network of friends or siblings. Either way, this group of one or more people raises the probability that you will do what you say you do. Knowing you will face the herd is what empowers you to face your oppressors.

Advocacy

It is simple to find people to attend your *celebration*; the real test is locating people who show up at your moment of *devastation*. Your herd consists of the caliber of people who walk into the room when the rest of the world walks out. Your herd is comprised of folks who advocate for you at your weakest, most desperate moments. Solomon describes a true supporter as one who "helps you up when you fall." This kind of support shows up when you "fall" into depression, addiction, financial destitution, moral decay or are simply stuck in an unhealthy relationship.

Perhaps the quintessential story from sports history that illustrates this kind of advocacy involves the friendship between Jackie Robinson, the first African-American to play Major League Baseball, and white-southerner Pee Wee Reese. During one game in Boston, an era when minorities had fastballs thrown at their heads and spikes on the bases, Jackie Robinson stood at home-plate waiting to hit the ball. The Caucasian crowd hurled their racial vulgarities as he stood there feeling completely alone. Noticing the sad sight, Pee Wee Reese left the dugout, stood next to Robinson with his arms draped over his shoulders and faced the angry crowd. Your herd consists of people who will stand alongside you to face your opposition.

Comradery

You have heard it said, "Misery loves company." But it's even worse than that when dealing with toxic people.

In toxic relationships, misery doesn't love company.
Misery demands hostages.

One of the most treacherous outcomes of a toxic-relationship is that your world becomes smaller and smaller. Your socializing becomes less and less. Your friends become fewer and fewer. In many cases, the insecurities of the ASS causes them to withdraw from relationships while taking you with them for the lonely ride. Tragically, you become a prisoner locked away with them in their lonely dungeon.

The idea of leaving the ASS might be grueling because you might not have any relationships left in your life. Over the last several months or years of being involved in a toxic-relationship, you may have defriended many people. Interestingly enough, a hormone in your brain known as oxytocin causes you to yearn for bonding with someone. These yearnings are so intense that if you were deserted on an island with not a soul in sight, you would take your volleyball, transform it into your best-friend and name it, Wilson. Make no mistake about it, without the ASS in your life, you just might turn your volleyball into a lover of sorts too.

Therefore, it is crucial for you to join a herd for the sake of comradery. When you make a break from your dangerous love, your emotional survival will hinge on having people who listen to your feelings, make you laugh, bring sunshine on a cloudy day and offer you a sense of belonging.

When lying down in such a frigid world, your herd will "keep you warm" (Ecclesiastes 4:11). The herd offers you a comradery that releases oxytocin within the brain, a feeling that assures your soul that you are not alone.

Safety

Being in a toxic-relationship is like living in a battle zone. It should be no surprise that studies have indicated that the effects of a long-term abusive relationship on the brain are similar to the neurological consequences of being in war. Both survivors of long-term abuse (physical, emotional and sexual) and veterans of war develop the symptoms of Post-Traumatic Stress Disorder (PTSD)—anxiety, hypervigilance, depression and a host of other symptoms. Your sense of safety, theorized by Abraham Maslow to be one of the most fundamental needs of human nature, is grossly compromised from living in such a hazardous circumstance for an extended period of time.

Joining a herd satisfies one of your most fundamental needs—the yearning for safety. The wise King Solomon tells us in Proverbs 11:14 almost exactly what we read in Ecclesiastes 4:12: "In the multitude of counsel, there is safety." According to Solomon, the godly counsel provided by the herd settles your fears, wanes your worries, and makes you feel protected.

Aside from emotional safety, the herd also offers you physical safety by navigating you out of dark places. The guidance of the herd could save your life from all sorts of dangerous outcomes. Let me break it down for you like this. Being in a toxic-relationship is like living in a pitch-black room with no electricity. In that dark room, you can't see clearly what you are dealing with. In that dark room, you are susceptible to further abuse at the hands of your captors. Somewhere in that room, there lies a window with the shades pulled down. When you pull up the shades, you permit the light from the outside to dispel the darkness on the inside. Seeking counsel from people, a.k.a. joining the herd, is like pulling up the shades—you permit the light from the outside to dispel the darkness on the inside. Alone, you might be overpowered by the darkness, but with the guidance of a partner, you can defend yourself.

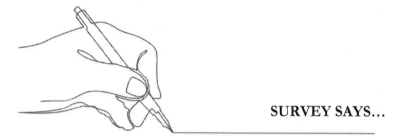

SURVEY SAYS...

Notes from our "Staying Close To The Herd" survey:
Here's what those who LEFT the relationship said:

Ani's herd served as her lifeline; her family, friends and pastors satisfied all four standards of Ecclesiastes 4. According to Ani, "My herd held me accountable. They would check in on me if they hadn't heard from me. They would probe if anything felt "off" about me. They would call me out on my silence, and sometimes my humor, discerning when I was being "avoidant." I also had friends in that herd that I could walk in their house, collapse on their couch and chat for hours while our little ones ran around the house. These relationships were medicine to my soul, and because of them, I hardly ever felt alone."

Stan says that without his herd, he wouldn't have been able to see straight. He says, "When I fell in love with my wife, I lost my eyesight. Being blinded by affection, it took me a while to see that she abused me regularly even to the point of being punched in the face. She ended the eighteen-year relationship with an affair. It was the gentle prodding of friends that inspired me to question her unexplainable lapses of time, sexy lingerie underneath her work outfits and unwarranted hostility. You just don't discern these realities when they are so close, no more than a fish can define water."

Conversely, *Meg's* experiences were partly the result of having the wrong people in her corner; folks that didn't live up to the standards of a herd. She says, "I ended up resenting them for intruding and not respecting the fact that I was living a nightmare." Sadly, Meg only had a handful of pastors who prayed and counseled her from a distance within her herd.

Remo states, "I actually had to look outside the church for my network of support. I mean, there were a few lay people but church folk don't always get these complicated situations. Oftentimes, church folk have a very narrow lens when it comes to divorce. They can be more concerned about what statement your divorce will make than they care about the fact that you were pushed out of a car going 50 mph. I actually found lots of help from my psychiatrist who not only helped me with my depression but navigate through the divorce. Of course, I felt a need to draw closer to my godly parents who held my hand throughout it all."

Here's what those who STAYED the relationship but broke free from toxic dynamics said:

Vilma says, "My husband entered into a network of men—*Marked Men For Christ*—that truly got to know him and held him accountable. I thank the Lord every day for such a rich group of men that not only came alongside my husband but also me. They wrapped around our family and continue to do so to this day. I have deep and wonderful relationships with many of the wives as well. They have shown us what it means to be completely transparent and unashamed, as well as how to walk with one another through the inevitable trials that come."

Paul says, "The Lord surrounded us with healthy hearted people who had not only heavenly perspectives but were able and available to help lead us into the truth. We made ourselves accountable to these authentic relationships and wholeheartedly implemented their support strategies."

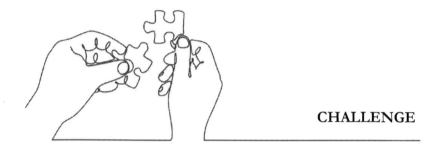

CHALLENGE

Putting the pieces together: The "Staying Close To The Herd" Challenge.

- Seek outside support by seeing a therapist, joining a support group (such as Al Anon) and becoming a part of a church family.
- Meet with someone you trust on a regular basis on the telephone, out for coffee, or wherever you feel comfortable.
- Don't just *show up*, but *open up!* Allow that trusted person into the private areas of your life. Share your struggles in this relationship with them. Unveil the good, the bad and the ugly.
- Don't just *open up*, but *listen up!* Give that person permission to shoot straight with you, ask you hard questions and challenge you on setting goals and keeping your commitments.

CHAPTER SEVEN
Pen Up

"However, if it was known that the Ox had the habit of goring, yet the owner did not keep it penned up, the owner must pay, animal for animal, and take the dead animal in exchange" (Exodus 21:36).

ARE YOU FED UP?

Even the OX, the most selfless animal on the farm, gets fed up and starts goring. When an OX gores, it utilizes its horns to jab or stab whatever crosses its path. The animal vents the frustrations of shouldering its heavy load upon whatever shows up in its vicinity. When the OX has gotten into the habit of goring, you know he/she has reached his boiling point. Even the kindest creatures have their limits.

Are you in the habit of goring? Perhaps you snap at every person who farts in the wrong direction. Your kids say you're a witch and the people at work call you something else that rhymes with *Witch* but starts with a *B*.

The longer you stay in this toxic situation, the more you despise the grouchy person you're morphing into. All of this goring means one thing—it means you are *fed up!*

Goring will not solve your problems. Sure, you could puncture your partner's eardrums with a number 2 pencil, but then you would have a bloody mess to clean up. And maybe even a domestic assault charge on your record. Who needs such aggravation? Unfortunately, by lashing out at others, we take slashes at ourselves. Galatians 5:15 says, "But if you keep on biting and devouring each other, watch out that you are not consumed by one another."

Many years ago, there was an animal in the wilderness known as the saber-tooth tiger. The animal's extinction left many scientists puzzled as to the reasons it disappeared from the earth. Then, one day, they found the fossils of two saber-tooth tigers biting into each other's face. Evidently, their extinction was the outcome of years of in-fighting. Make no mistake about it, the habit of goring will only result in your destruction. You can't hurt someone else without also destroying yourself.

If you are *goring*, it means you are *fed up* from shouldering a series of heavy loads. You've had just about enough! Even the nicest people have their limits.

**When you are FED UP,
It's an indication that it's time to PEN UP!**

The Pen

A pen is an enclosure for animals that shelters them from other beasts and shields other beasts from them. Inside the pen, animals are afforded the opportunity to calm down, collect themselves and find rest for their irritable selves. Without the pen, animals would become either erratic or robotic from spending too much time in the same contentious environment. Erratic animals are dangerously aggressive while robotic animals are tragically subservient. Erratic animals have the will to kill while robotic animals have killed their will. Both are the outcome of never taking any space from their warzone.

Just like the OX, you are in desperate need of a pen! Inside your pen, you have the chance to unwind, reflect and reconvene with your Savior. Without your pen, you run the risk of becoming erratic and lashing out at someone else. Or, you become robotic and lose yourself. Either one of these extremes bring out the worse in your personality; the side of you that Carl

Jung calls "the shadow"...Freud identifies as "the id"...the neuroscientists call "survival instincts" and the Bible calls "the flesh." Many folks have committed atrocities simply because they were exhaustingly needful of a pen.

A pen is an actual place that affords you space from your warzone.

Consider the natural pens that God built within creation for animals to find shelter during times of vulnerability. When a bear needs rest, it unearths a cave. When a caterpillar comes undone, it builds a cocoon. When a fox requires replenishment, it digs a hole. Even Jesus, the All-Sufficient One, had pens all throughout his neighborhood where He refueled. Luke 5:16 states: "Yet, He frequently withdrew to lonely places..." Some may argue that Jesus had no pen based on His statement in Matthew 8:20, "Foxes have holes, the birds of the air have nests but the Son of Man has no place to lay His head." But this statement is not a reflection of Him having no place to hide but having no spot on this earth to permanently reside.

Below, you will find a list of possible pens where you can retreat from your warzone in order to unwind and reconvene with God.

1. A natural setting

Some people find a spot under a walnut tree, or a blanket at the beach, or a cave in the mountains to getaway. In an ecopsychology study of 20,000 people conducted by the European Centre for Environment and Human Health at the University of Exeter, it was found that people who spend two hours per day outdoors reported substantially better physical and psychological health outcomes. Immersion in nature results in the reduction of muscle tension, heart disease, the production of cortisol (stress hormones) and an overall better mood.

2. A visit with your friend

Others find reprieve over a cup of coffee with a friend at a local café or their home. The Swedish Proverb stands true, "Shared joy is double joy. Shared sorrow is half a sorrow."

3. Church

Wise people find their refuge in the House of God. In addition to all of the benefits listed in the Bible of assembling with the saints, growing research emerges on the benefits of church which include decrease in depression, a protective factor against substance abuse, elevation of self-efficacy levels and a mediating factor in handling emotional distress.

4. Long-drives in your car

Tracy Chapman's hit-song from the 1980's, "Fast Cars" captures the thoughts and feelings of someone getting behind the wheel to escape from their pain. *Medical News Study* reported a Brazilian study on how long drives accompanied by music reduce stress.

5. Nostalgic places

Trips through old neighborhoods, schoolyards and other sentimental territory can remind you of how far God has taken you. These settings encourage us by saying, "If you made it through hell and highwater then, you will make it again!" Take heed by picking places that inspire you; some places could trigger trauma, digging your hole of despair even deeper.

6. The bathroom

This may sound silly, but some people find it impossible to leave their home for various reasons. I know a lady who fit such a criteria, and admitted that sitting on her shaggy pink rug inside of her bathroom served as her sanctuary.

In summary, it is impossible to heal in the same environment that hurts you. A regular reprieve is vital to the survival of your soul. Therefore, find a suitable pen(s) that you can withdraw to frequently for peace of mind. Also, by retreating to this pen regularly, you are reminding your soul that your hazardous environment is not your true habitat. You may be *in* those surroundings but you are not *of* those surroundings. If you are fed up, it's time to pen up.

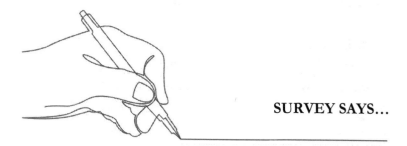

SURVEY SAYS...

Notes from our "Penning Up" survey:
Here's what those who LEFT the relationship said:

Meg says, "For the last twelve years of the marriage, we didn't share a bed. I slept on the couch while he stayed in our bedroom. That humble couch kept me from feeling defiled by him, especially in light of the infidelity. That couch was my pen."

Stan says, "I would hide in my office, locking the door behind me. For some reason, being surrounded by my desk, my books and my computer, reminded me that God had bigger purposes for me than being her husband. Also, a drive to New York City, just a couple of hours away, assured my soul that I was a free-agent, quite capable of leaving whenever I wanted to."

Ani says, "I'd visit my girlfriend, collapse on her couch and unload my emotional laundry while our little ones ran around the house with their dolls. My friendships were my solace. Also, believe it or not, reading a book gave me wings to escape. I found my pen in whatever book I was reading. He was actually jealous of the fact that I could rise above our chaos through a book while he needed substance."

Remo says, "First and foremost, the prayer closet. After that, the time I spent with my girls was my refuge. I can't tell you how many excursions we went on alone even during the marriage. But that time with them was the best distraction from the madness I could ever experience."

Here's what those who STAYED within the relationship but broke free from toxic dynamics said:

Paul says, "One of the newer practices I've learned has been to be still, sit and simply listen in the secret place. I have several secret places of prayer. I've always ventured into my Christianity with a zeal to know, grow and show which can be exhausting and that performance based theology can leave me empty and dry. The truth is I have, and am all that I need, simply and childlike in Him."

Vilma says, "Many times I would just drive and pray. Just get in my car, unpack what I felt and seek God. We had a couple we could reach out to during those moments, which proved to be very helpful. The wife would hear me out and help lead me out of my emotions and back into the truth."

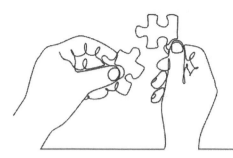

Putting the pieces together: The "Pen Up" Challenge.

- Find a Pen that fits the following criteria: some distance from your warzone, connotes feelings of safety and warmth, and is easily accessible.
- Frequent your Pen at least three times in one week, and every time you feel fed up.
- Keep your Pen a secret!

CHAPTER EIGHT

Do What's Under-Your-Nose

"For my yoke is easy, and my burden is light" (Matthew 11:30).

AN EASY YOKE

The only yoke beneficial to wear in this life is the *easy yoke* that Jesus promises in Matthew 11:30. In farming, an *easy yoke* was descriptive of the yoke that a weak animal bore when joined together with a stronger beast. It was called an *easy yoke* because the weak animal accomplished the easy things while the strong animal did all of the brunt work. In our culture, we would say when someone had an easy job to fulfill in some contractual agreement, "he or she got the easy end of the deal."

In Matthew 11:30, wearing an *easy yoke* means coming into relationship with Jesus Christ who assumes responsibility for all of the hard work in your life. An *easy yoke* means you are the weak animal while He is the stronger one, taking care of the stuff too heavy for you. Hence is the reason why Jesus is prophetically described as the ultimate "OX" in Ezekiel 1:10. He's quite capable of bearing the burdens too heavy for us to carry.

God assumes full responsibility for the Soul that entrusts itself to him

Are you stressed out right now? As they say in Al-Anon, *Easy Does It!* Trust Jesus with all the matters too much for your mind to grasp while you simply obey Him in whatever lies before you. Yes, you play a role in being healthy and holy, but that role is relegated to what lies within your sphere of control. In the words of Oswald Chambers, "God will do whatever you can't do, but refuses to do what He's constructed you to do."

The stuff *over-your-head*
Versus the stuff *under-your-nose*

Too often, you worry about the stuff *over-your-head*. The phrase, *over-your-head* is descriptive of situations too complex for you to handle. *Over-your-head* refers to the circumstances beyond your control and impossible for you to fix, manage or even address. When you break free from a toxic-relationship, there will be a list of *over-your-head* circumstances to obsess about. For instance:

1. Others' reactions
2. Others' perception of you
3. Past events
4. Future events
5. Sickness or death
6. Money you don't have
7. Physical or mental handicaps
8. Being alone
9. Nature
10. Your Personality

Any attempt to change the stuff *over-your-head* is as stupid as trying to get from point A to point B while running on a treadmill. You expend lots of energy, yet you get nowhere. What are the *over-your-head* matters right now you are worried about? Write a list of those items in order to come back to that list in six months from now.

In a study conducted by behavioral scientists a few years back, a group of participants were asked to write a list of the things they worried about. After an extended period of time, it was proven that 85% of those dreadful scenarios never materialized. The delusion of worry is that renders the slimmest possibilities into guaranteed realities within our minds. Through the worrisome lens, events that are unlikely appear to be inevitable. An additional finding of this study revealed that most of the 15% of the *over-your-head* scenarios that did occur were far more bearable than what they imagined them to be. Therefore, the anticipation of the event was far worse than its actualization. Worry proves to be, not only practically useless, but emotionally reckless.

"My life has been filled with terrible misfortunes; most of which never happened"
—*Michel de Montaigne*

Now, let's talk about the stuff *under-your-nose*. The *under-your-nose* stuff pertains to the matters that reside within your sphere of control. One of the problems with obsessing about the stuff *over-your-head* is that it plunders all of your energy, leaving you too exhausted to do the stuff *under-your-nose*. Below, you will find a list of examples of matters within your sphere of control.

1. How you treat others
2. How you perceive situations
3. How you react to people, places, and things
4. The places you go
5. The people you visit
6. The things you digest
7. The help you seek or don't seek
8. Your thoughts
9. Your words

10. How you spend your resources (including time)

When you do what's *under-your-nose*, you will often discover that what's *over-your-head* will work itself out; or I should say, God will work it out. Often times, we dismiss the task under our nose because it seems so small in comparison to the mountains before us. But small strides make big differences in the grand scheme of things. For instance, every mountain entail grains of dust, every year consists of 31,536,000 seconds and every exodus from a toxic-relationship involves a series of small steps.

Never underestimate the
Significance of each miniature step
You take towards freedom.

The Story of Robert the Bruce

Legend claims that during the 1300s, Robert the Bruce, the King of Scotland, took refuge in a cave as he was being hunted down by a pursuer. Shortly after he entered, Divine Providence inspired a spider to form a web at the entrance of the cave. When the pursuer arrived, he saw the spider web dangling from the mouth of the cave. The sight of this small spectacle misled him to believe that Robert the Bruce couldn't have taken cover inside without breaking the web. The pursuer quickly left that spot, unwittingly leaving Robert the Bruce safely inside the cave. Imagine, the destiny of Robert the Bruce and his millions of followers hinged on the small gestures of a spider.

Perhaps you feel so powerless right now in breaking free from your domestic bondage. Quite possibly you have exhausted yourself in mulling over the stuff *over-your-head*. Just be obedient to what God would want you to do with the stuff *under-your-nose*—no matter how trifling it may seem—and He will take care of stuff *over-your-head*. Remember...

Big events, like breaking free from a toxic-relationship, hinge on a sequence of small acts.

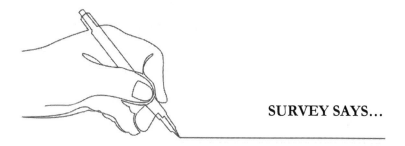

SURVEY SAYS...

Notes from our "Do what's under-your-nose" survey:
Here's what those who LEFT the relationship said:

Ani states, "I learned that my peace and happiness are my own, and I have a measure of control over those mindsets regardless of other's actions. I learned that other feelings are mine to manage as well. By taking responsibility for these things, I took the power away from my partner."

Stan states, "Looking back, it's amazing how many mountains God moved on my behalf. Financial hardship, a place to live, new relationships—so many blessings unfolded that made the leaving a little easier. But nothing moved until I made a move! It was on me to ask my aunt to sleep on her couch, pack up my stuff, leave the house and even file the paper-work for divorce after praying for months for her to turn from the adulterous relationship."

Meg states, "At some point, it dawned on me that he wasn't keeping me in this situation—I was. I helped create and participate this insane situation. I took responsibility for my codependency. From that point, I was able to make all the miniscule logistic decisions to end the raw deal I signed up for."

Remo states, "Being consistent in the small things. Keeping my routine regardless of my depression. Showing up for church every Sunday, continuing in my job and my school work, being present at board meetings, etc. I was in need of big miracles, but I'm a firm believer that miracles only happen when you are making forward movement."

Here's what those who STAYED within the relationship but broke free from toxic dynamics said:

Vilma says, "My husband and I made the decision to be accountable to other people which was something that has changed the entire landscape of our marriage. By learning to allow trustworthy people in who had walked through their own healings, we were consistently coached to keep our eyes on ourselves and walk in forgiveness. Through that we both learned to deal with our own hearts and our own responses, despite what the other person was doing. That paved the way to healing the wounds that resided in us from before we were even married."

Paul says, "My biggest micro decision was based on the scripture in Psalms "Early I will seek Thee." For me, this didn't mean waking up at the crack of dawn to do my devotions, but to seek Him and His will in advance on all decisions, dilemmas, and despairs. The Holy Spirit began to fill me with wisdom and discernment, first, intuitively into myself yet also circumstantially. My reactions changed dramatically."

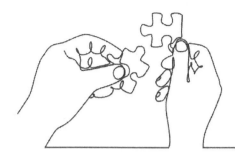

Putting the pieces together: The "Do what's under-your-nose" Challenge.

- Make a list of the stuff "Under-Your-Nose" and the stuff "Over-Your-Head."
- Say the "Serenity Prayer" in the morning before you head out and at night before you go to sleep.
- When you catch yourself worrying, write the object of your worry on a piece of paper, and rip it up.
- Anticipate mountains moving as you manage what lies within your sphere of control. Document each mountain cast into the sea on your behalf.

CHAPTER NINE
Outgrow Your Oppressor

"In that day, the burden will be lifted from your shoulder and their yoke from your neck; the yoke will be broken because you have grown so fat"
(Isaiah 10:27).

THE COST OF GROWTH

If you've ever seen the 2001 film, *I Am Sam*, you probably remember the moment when the social worker determines that it would be better for ten-year-old Lucy to live with someone other than her mentally challenged father, Sam (portrayed by Sean Penn).

This decision is based on the projection that Lucy will stop developing socially and intellectually once she reaches the same echelon as her father.

It is a human tendency to stay in step with those around us; hence the meaning of Proverbs 13:20: "Walk with the wise and become wise. Associate with fools and get in trouble."

In order to set Lucy up for boundless growth, the social worker mandates a new placement that's suitable for her potential.

It is very difficult, and almost impossible, for a person to outgrow the people whom they bond with. Fish will not outgrow the size of their bowl; neither will a person allow themselves to surpass the level of their partners.

Researchers at the University of California concluded that growth often results in the forfeiture of people, places and things that are not moving on the same upward trajectory. We stop growing because the cost of growth means loss...and we are *petrified* of loss.

When you choose to grow, whatever around you that doesn't want to GROW typically has to GO.

Ponder for a moment how you've been stunted in your growth by accommodating your partner. I know a lady who walked away from a successful career as an attorney because it intimidated her husband. I know a young man who dropped his college courses because his girlfriend felt sad without him. I know another man who stopped attending church because his faith in God exacerbated his wife's animosity towards God. What opportunities have you declined? To what did you say *No* that you really wanted to say, *Yes*? What did you forfeit all because you weren't willing to pay the cost of growth—the loss of people, places and things that refuse to grow with you?

Leaving the ASSES behind

In Genesis 22:5, Abraham resolves to ascend a particular mountain in order to meet with God. Before he starts climbing, he says to his servant, "Stay here with the asses while I go worship God." When you make a decision to climb any mountain, you have to be willing to leave the asses behind. The asses may have accompanied Abraham to where he was, but they weren't built for where he was going. An ass would have probably fainted from exhaustion after a few feet of climbing. Similarly, there are people who accompanied you throughout all your history, but that does not mean they are spiritually, mentally and emotionally fit to handle your destiny. Oftentimes, climbing the mountain involves a willingness to leave the asses behind.

Don't get this twisted—the decision to grow does not necessarily mean a resolution to leave your partner. In the case of Abraham and the asses, Abraham did not abandon the asses forever; rather, he left them behind for the period it would take him to scale the mountain. If the asses left during his ascension, it was their choice to leave and not Abraham's. In the same way, if you resolve to climb some mountain, you are not abandoning your partner. If they choose to leave you because of your decision, you did not abandon them…they forsook you.

Outgrow your oppressors

In Isaiah 10:27, the yoke of bondage breaks when the OX's neck becomes fat. A fat neck is indicative of a matured animal; a beast that decided to grow. The prophet Isaiah teaches us that your growth brings about your breakthrough. If you are having a difficult time breaking free from something, just grow a little more. At some point, your soul will become so big that the yoke linking you with that ASS will snap.

When you can't get rid of your oppressors, outgrow them!

Choosing to grow may include one or more of the following paths. This is not an exhaustive list but a few examples of personal development.

1. Enroll in a course
2. Join the gym
3. Become a member of a church family
4. Attend a support group
5. Find a therapist
6. Go on a mission trip

7. Take up an engaging hobby like dancing, music, art classes, joining a choir, learning a foreign language, etc.

Here's a little foresight on what happens with your relationships when you choose to grow. Below, you will find three likely reactions from the ASSES in your life, all of which benefit you in the long run.

1. Your Growth MOTIVATES Your Partner.

In the best-case scenario, your growth motivates your partner to make necessary changes in their own life in order to become a better person. By doing so, they undergo the metamorphosis of an ASS into an OX. This may sound like a ridiculous notion, but miracles do happen. Your growth may actually inspire change in your partner. At the same time, don't resolve to grow for that reason lest you should become discouraged by poor results. Resolve to grow simply for the sake of your *own* soul.

2. Your Growth INFURIATES Your Partner.

If your partner is deeply insecure, your growth will only infuriate them because it highlights their own inadequacy. Like juxtaposing a blemished cloth with a pure white cloth, the blemishes appear so much dirtier when placed side by side with the white cloth. In the same fashion, your positive changes accentuate their negative behavior. This contrast often induces shame which morphs into anger towards you. If this happens, your growth in confidence and wisdom will enable you to respond appropriately. In some cases, their infuriation will give you the grounds to leave.

3. Your Growth ELIMINATES Them.

If your partner fears being deserted, there's a likelihood that they will forsake you when you resolve to grow. Your growth smells like abandonment, and they will leave you to dodge the agony of being abandoned by you. In these cases, their absence will probably cause enormous grief. But if you work through your grief (Google the *Kubler-Ross Model* to understand the stages of grief), you will eventually come to a place of *relief*. You will look back at some point…in relief…of being delivered from such a toxic situation.

When you are stuck in a toxic-relationship, too much time and energy is squandered in trying to change, fix, heal, rescue or help your partner. These endeavors are as foolish as trying to motivate an ASS to run a marathon. It would be much wiser to channel all that time and energy into your own personal development. In the process of growing, you will find that the yoke between you and the ASS will snap off because it cannot accommodate how massive your soul has become.

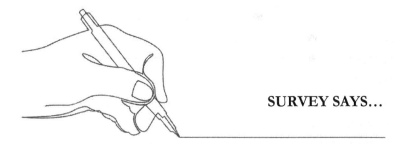

SURVEY SAYS…

Notes from our "Outgrowing Your Oppressor" survey:
Here's what those who LEFT the relationship said:

Meg states, "When I first met him, I was severely depressed. During that bleak era, his childish behaviors were a fun escape from my plight. But when our daughter was born, adulting was required. The birth of my daughter made me grow up. I maintained a good job while he played his silly games. I grew spiritually and adulted in all the ways that kept the fort down. The more I grew, the less challenging or appealing he was to me. I just disliked him more and more."

Remo states, "I grew in my self-esteem. That alone changed everything. Accomplishments such as several college degrees, the starting of multiple business enterprises and the approval I felt from God gave me leverage over her abuse. The more I grew in that area, the easier it was to stomach her rejection. When you know your worth, you don't need anyone else to price it for you."

Stan says, "I read books, attended seminars, traveled any chance I got, developed a worldview that transcended my miserable circumstances. At the risk of sounding arrogant, I started to feel like I lived on a higher plane than her insanity. In fact, every time she went low with some insult or abuse, I went high. I was able to ignore her because my mind was on better things."

Ani states, "I outgrew my oppressor mainly through my relationship with God. The closer I drew to Him, the more I acquired the emotional maturity to handle conflicts. When we would argue, I found myself swearing and yelling less and less. He was all alone in the feuds. I was actually able to turn the cheek, walk away and find a place to pray. Also, my boundaries were getting better and better. Pretty soon, we were miles apart in maturity. Also, I preoccupied myself with nature, photography, exploring new places, fun activities and reading. My interests were growing beyond my previous obsession with him."

Here's what those who STAYED within the relationship but broke free from toxic dynamics said:

Vilma says, "There were times that I was moving forward in ministry when my husband was not and this created an underlying tension that at times triggered his feelings of inadequacy and fears that I wouldn't put him first. This was something I didn't notice initially as it didn't surface in extreme behaviors, but over time we learned to have great discussion about it and process it together."

Paul says, "At times I felt light years ahead, but at other times, felt like I was in the Stone Age. At times, our growth replicated each other's while at other times, we circled around each other. For me, this caused some frustration as we were being aligned in different ways but also created a well of hope and inspiration."

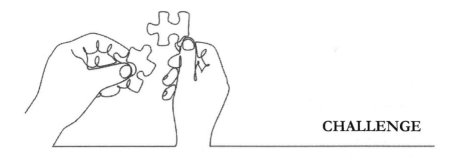

CHALLENGE

Putting the pieces together: The "Outgrow Your Oppressor" Challenge.

- Identify the areas of personal development where you feel stuck and identify paths that will lead you out.
- Take a step down that particular path whether it means inquiring for information, enrollment, etc. Do what you need to do to get that ball rolling!
- Take casual notice of how your growth affects your relationships. Keep moving forward despite any resistance you face.

CHAPTER TEN

Nurse Your Wounds

"He heals the broken-hearted, and binds up their wounds"
(Psalm 147:3).

SHARK PREY

An open wound in shark-infested water turns any mammal into automatic prey. A shark can smell blood from up to a quarter mile away—blood scent molecules will travel over that distance and actually dissolve into the lining of the shark's nose. The safest measure that a mammal can take against shark attack is to make sure their wounds are healed before entering shark territory. An open lesion is an invitation to destruction. In the same manner, your psychological wounds are an allure to predators of various kinds when you enter the dating scene again.

According to Dr. Loren Soeiro, there are four types of predators to look out for.

- The *anti-social narcissist*...the badass who is extremely difficult, self-centered and anti-establishment. A wounded soul's attraction to this type often relates to its need to feel protected by this badass figure.
- The *prosocial narcissist*...the loud, gregarious personality that draws in the world with its charisma. A wounded soul's pull towards this type often relates to its need to glean and rely on their social genius.
- The *vulnerable narcissist*...the chronically victimized person who needs constant rescuing. A wounded soul's magnetism to this type often relates to their need to focus on someone else's pain in order to deflect from their own.

- The *malignant narcissist*...the downright abusive person who verbally and sometimes physically attacks you early on. A wounded soul's magnetism towards this type relates to its need for approval from the one who plays hard to get.

Your knack to detect the danger of these personalities when you are wounded is as strong as your ability to discern the threat of a cannoli when you are starving. In both cases, the discernment and resistance is very weak. Therefore, the best measure you can take is to allow your wounds the time needed to heal before entering the dating game. In Psalm 147:3, the Psalmist speaks about God binding up your wounds, illustrative of the ointment and bandages that a farmer uses when remedying an animal's abrasions. An animal has no business entering the wild until its wounds have been remedied. Let's discuss some of the afflictions that incur from being in a toxic-relationship.

Wounds and remedies

Involvement in a toxic-relationship for an extended period of time will often cause one of more of the following afflictions of the soul. Alongside each wound, you will also find a corresponding remedy. Of course, all of these remedies must be saturated with prayer and the Word of God.

1. Broken Trust...*Defining the wound:*
Trust has been defined by psychologists as the "lubricant of social interaction" that keeps relationships running smoothly. When your trust has been damaged by some calloused soul, it is like having all of your lubricant depleted. Trust damaged here

results in trust broken everywhere. When you're out of lubricant, your social interactions with people becomes jaded by timidity, cynicism, fear of rejection and a host of other toxic emotions. David's trust was broken in Psalm 88:18 when he cried, "You have made my loved ones and companions distant. Darkness is my only friend."

Remedy: Since it was a relationship that broke your trust, it will be relationships that will rebuild your trust. God often uses the stuff that broke us as the tools to build us. By cultivating relationships with family, friends and even a future mate when the time is right, your sense of confidence in yourself and others will be restored within these relationships. Many psychologists recommend adopting an animal such as a dog, cat or even a horse when your trust in people has been shattered. Bonding with these animals can rebuild your trust.

2. Shattered Self-Image...*Defining the wound:*

A shattered self-image is like gazing into one of those warped mirrors in a fun house whereby your deplorable attributes are accentuated (e.g. a big nose becomes colossal or a double-chin looks like a giant misshapen potato) while your adorable qualities are downplayed. Toxic partners have a way of tainting our own perception of ourselves by subtly, and sometimes blatantly, pointing out what's wrong with us.

The danger of a shattered self-image is that it affects the way we behave. Solomon warns about this phenomenon in Proverbs 23:7 when he says, "As a person thinks in their heart, so they become."

Remedy: Write a list of positive attributes about yourself as well as a list of areas of improvement. Make sure for every area of improvement, you write down two positive attributes. When you are finished, read the list to a trusted friend. Ask that friend for their feedback on each attribute, and write down their responses.

3. Weakened Self-efficacy...*Defining the wound:*

Self-efficacy is your own confidence in your ability to perform a task successfully as well produce positive results from whatever task you perform.

Toxic partners plant seeds of self-doubt within your mind, causing you to question your ability to do anything right. Through words of criticism, or even gaslighting tactics, you lose your confidence in your ability to manage a checkbook, hold down a job, clean the house, drive a car or even think independently. Oftentimes, toxic partners attack your self-efficacy in order to keep you dependent upon them; their manipulative way of remaining on the throne of your heart. The Psalmist describes this weakened self-efficacy when he's no longer capable of singing his songs. He says in Psalm 22:15, "My tongue sticks to the roof of my mouth."

Remedy: One of the most effective ways of rebuilding your self-efficacy is generating a list of goals—short-term and long-term.

Even a daily agenda with a list of items to do strengthens your self-efficacy. As you complete a task, no matter how small it is, check it off your list. The sight of a finished tasks—small or big—reminds us of our capability. Also, make time to celebrate any of your monumental accomplishments.

4. Post-Traumatic Stress...*Defining the wound:*

As mentioned earlier, studies have shown that people involved in a toxic-relationship for an extended period of time develop the same post-traumatic stress symptoms as soldiers coming home from war. These symptoms include anxiety, hyper-vigilance, harassing flashbacks and even fits of rage. When stress is no longer a temporary state but a lasting trait, you may have developed Post-Traumatic Stress Disorder. The Psalmist may have suffered from this disorder as evident in Psalm 22:16 when he says, "Dogs surround me, and a pack of villains encircle me."

Remedy: Albeit I'm deeply biased, I strongly recommend my book, *Pen Your Pain Into Parables* alongside working with a therapist in order to process through the traumas you have suffered.

5. The Disease of Resentment...*Defining the wound:*

When resentment infects the soul, you suffer from fixations with the wrongs committed against you. Obsessive thoughts about the atrocities you suffered permeate your mind, often accompanied by an insatiable desire to get even. This resentful thinking usually interrupts other relationships too, making enemies out of almost everyone. The disciples exhibited this resentment towards the Samaritans in Luke 9:54 when they wanted to call fire down from heaven to destroy a Samaritan village for not welcoming them.

Remedy: The only true remedy for resentment is a process called forgiveness. All of the steps involved in forgiveness purge the soul of all acrimony you feel towards your offender. The steps of forgiveness include the following:

First, acknowledge the nature and gravity of the wrongs committed against you. Resist the temptation to minimize those wrongs by saying, "Well, they didn't mean it" or "It wasn't that bad." These statements are forms of denial that keep your ill-feelings bottled up. Forgiveness must always begin with acknowledging the offense. When Joseph forgave his brothers in Genesis, he starts out with saying, "The evil you committed against me…" He made no excuses for their wrongs, but named it what it was—evil.

Second, articulate the feelings that resulted from those wrongs to God and someone you trust. For example, you may say, "I was hurt by what happened" or 'I felt confused." Once again, the book, *Pen Your Pain Into Parables* is a helpful tool with accessing your pent-up feelings.

Third, think about what you believe your offender owes you. For instance, you may even feel the need to get even with them in some way. Chances are, you are justifiable in what you believe is owed to you.

Fourth, cancel the debts owed to you. The term, "forgive" in the New Testament is actually a financial word that means, "To cancel a debt." From this point forward, you have no right to hold that person's wrongs over their head lest you should fall back into resentment. The cancelation of the debt may be something you communicate to the offender, or may remain between you and God.

6. Early Childhood Wounds…*Defining the wound:*

These particular wounds pre-date your relationship with the ASS, finding their roots in the formative years of your life at the hands of your caretakers. Nonetheless, these wounds played an imperative role in your relationship with the ASS, and will inevitably influence your future relationships unless you experience healing. For instance, maybe you never have received approval from your father or mother; hence, the stage was set for you to crave that lost affection from an ASS who offers you nothing more than rejection. Or your dysfunctional childhood might have marred your worldview, causing you to believe that abuse is tolerable, permissible and even normal. In many ways, the events of our early childhood leave us with wounds that catch the attention of sharks throughout our adult years.

Remedy: A therapist who specializes in Cognitive-Behavioral-Therapy (C.B.T), active involvement with a community of faith and a daily time of Bible reading is recommended. Also, once again, I would highly suggest turning to my book, *Pen Your Pain Into Parables* to work through the damage that's been done to your soul.

SURVEY SAYS...

Notes from our "Nursing Your Wounds" survey:
Here's what those who LEFT the relationship said:

Meg states, "My parents never showed affection. I knew they loved each other. I mean, they would kiss when he came home, he would pat her on the back. They were almost like Archie and Edith from *All In The Family* seated in the recliner and rocking chair. They were more like roommates. Ironically, I was told twice that I was a roommate by a man. Because my dad was emotionally unavailable, I went after men who were equally as cold. My childhood set me up to accept affectionless situations as the norm. Lots of my healing had to be with becoming comfortable with being loved and receiving affection."

Ani states, "My parents stayed with one another while not even liking each other. Then, after many years, they split while still remaining married. That set a pretty low standard of what marriage is supposed to be. Partly because of that, I stayed for many years even though I didn't like my ex-husband. But I think the real wounds I dealt with were from the marriage more than my childhood. I was never an anxious person in my life until suffering his abuse. I was always a social person, yet became isolated and distanced myself from many friends. My wounds today are an emotional blockage that keep me from getting close with anyone simply to avoid being hurt."

Stan says, "My mother was very critical of me, and it left me starving for her approval. It's no surprise that I spent many years of my marriage overly sensitive to my ex's approval. I remember sharing my dreams with her while she rolled her eyes. She didn't have to say much. Just a disdainful look, and she could crush me. Healing for me meant work on my inner child, and letting that wounded child find his approval in God…and of course, I needed healing from the rejection my ex inflicted upon me throughout the years. I remember feeling like nobody would ever want me after we divorced. My aunt had to tell me over and over, 'Stan, you are a hot commodity!' to feel better about myself."

Remo states, "My self-esteem was injured deeply in both my childhood and marriage. For instance, when your own wife is agreeable to sex with her less than ten times in decades of marriage, your manhood takes a beating. Also, financial setbacks. For a man, not having money takes a toll on the concept of yourself. These are areas in which I've made progress through counseling, and my walk with God, but it has been slow."

Here's what those who STAYED within the relationship but broke free from toxic dynamics said:

Vilma says, "My relationship wounded my sense of trust (in my spouse, God's plan, and the ability of the church to love in the ways of Christ). Seeing my husband heal began to restore my sense of trust in him. The Lord also told me clearly during that time that He was watching over the words that were spoken to my husband about our marriage to make sure that change would come to pass. I was brought deeper into a trust and understanding that my ways were not His ways and that as painful as it was, we surrendered to the process of uprooting things in our souls that needed to go. Healing came over time with total dependence on God's hand at work. My trust in the church was also restored with some of the new community that the Lord brought to us. As we experienced people being honest about their own difficulties we realized most couples struggle and can also find healing. We were also loved right where we were and for who we were not just who we could become."

Paul says, "When I got married, I thought many of my troubles would dissolve into a powerful package of holy matrimony and union. What actually happened is that all of my greatest fears and brokenness would now rise up rapidly to the surface of a true relationship. God, in His jealousy of a covenant began to work and rework the soul of my heart to remove any contaminants that remained. My wife did that as well, often not as gently and lovingly. This created a division in my mind that made me question some of the broken beliefs that created faulty foundations. Everything that I built either crumbled under my wobbly legs or catapulted me to a deeper faith. This actually began a sifting process for years that is still being ironed out daily but beautifully."

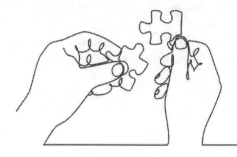

Putting the pieces together: The "The Nurse Your Wounds" Challenge.

- Identify the wounds in your life that have attracted sharks.
- Implement the suggested remedies for that particular wound or other remedies you have carefully researched.
- Apply the feedback you are receiving from those remedial measures.

CHAPTER ELEVEN
Know Your Owner

"The Ox knows its owner" (Isaiah 1:3).

YOU NEED A PARTNER,
NOT AN OWNER

When an ox knows its owner, the animal has no space in its soul for a second proprietor. When an ox builds a relationship with its owner, it refuses to offer itself to anyone else. Oxen desire other oxen to mate with, not to be possessed by or to possess.

Likewise, when a woman builds a relationship with her Lord and Savior, other relationships within her life are not dictatorships but partnerships.

When a woman knows her true owner, she becomes impervious to manipulative tactics practiced by those who seek to control her.

Also, when a man knows his owner, he seeks for a relationship with a woman not to be his mother but his lover. He also shows himself to be unyielding to the schemes of a domineering woman.

Conversely, toxic-relationships consist of controlling dynamics where one person possesses the other like an owner lords over his animals. Within these relationships, love is not the petroleum that fuels one person to serve the other.

Instead, the following methods of control make this happen within the relationship. All of these methods of control insinuate an oppressive relationship whereby a rulership exists instead of a partnership.

All of these measures are taken by one party to emotionally beat the other into submission.

- *Guilt Trips:* Toying with someone's conscience to get them to do what you want.
- *Fear-Tactics:* Implying threats of punishment and abandonment to ensure cooperation.
- *False Alarms:* Creating fictitious emergencies to capture someone's attention.
- *Stonewalling:* Intentionally giving someone the silent treatment or emotionally starving them in order to wear them down and turn them into a captive.

The most effective defense against these tactics is to "know your owner." By building a relationship with your God, a few things happen within your psyche. First, you will recognize when someone attempts to control you. Being in relationship with the owner of all creation opens your eyes to a spiritual reality hidden behind the veil of natural phenomenon. Within that reality, you will discern when God's seat on the throne of your heart is under threat by intruders who covet His authority.

Second, the Lord Himself will rise up within you (since He lives inside of you) and defend His rightful position as the only worthy monarch in your life. His uprising will manifest through a boldness that overtakes you within your interactions with your so-called partner. You may find yourself saying with a firm love that refuses to be trampled upon, "I cannot go along with that, lest it should grieve my God."

Right Foot/Left Foot Dynamics

Confusion about roles in a marriage often sets in when Bible verses such as I Corinthians 11:3 are mentioned. Throughout history, women were browbeaten into subservient status by men who misused the concept of "headship" to wield their authority over a woman's autonomy. (On a side-note, extreme teachings of feminism have produced the opposite outcome whereby men are reduced to robotic status programmed to nod "yes" to every request made by their woman. Once again, this kind of relationship is more of a rulership than a partnership.) This idea of "headship" is inaccurate in depicting what Paul meant in I Corinthians, and what Jesus demonstrated as head of the church. Allow me to use the relational dynamics between your two feet as a metaphor to illustrate headship in a relationship.

Science teaches us that we all have one particular foot that leads most of the time. Some people lead with their right foot whereas others lead with their left foot. Essentially, being the leading foot means that it goes "first." It is the first foot to step into the office or step out onto the dance floor. In the same way, if you assume the head position in your relationship, it means you go "first." Headship means you have the responsibility to apologize first when conflict erupts. Headship means the onus is placed upon you to humble yourself first, to love and serve first. Headship is not a luxury but a responsibility.

Let's continue with the feet analogy. After the leading foot makes the first move, it doesn't remain in a position of leadership over the secondary foot. If your leading foot insists upon always being the leading foot, your body would make slow progress. Why? Because you would be limping rather than walking. In a similar way, when a husband always insists upon being in front, his relationship "limps" rather than "walks." The oppressive man always hollering, *"Woman, stay behind me"* never makes the headway he could make if he learned the dynamics of leadership demonstrated by his own feet. The leading foot leads the way, but then gets out of the way for the secondary foot to lead the way. One foot submits to another as the body moves forward. In summary, good leaders don't produce followers; good leaders produce other leaders. And a good man makes room for his woman's soul to shine forth without being intimidated by her power.

SURVEY SAYS...

Notes from our "Knowing Your Owner" survey:
Here's what those who LEFT the relationship said:

Ani says, "My relationship with my Lord instilled in me a sense of worth. It was a gradual process but he was always reminding me of my value. It helped me feel like I belonged to Him and wasn't meant to be controlled by my ex. It caused me to look over and up, beyond my ex to what God wanted for me. He gave me people who valued me and saw me for who I was. People who genuinely loved and adored me even with my faults. His love gave me the confidence to walk away."

Meg says, "Knowing my owner meant that knowing I belonged to Him. For many years, I allowed my ex to control to me. But now I don't. He still tries every day to infiltrate and control from a distance through our daughter. But now, I know my Owner and the value he put on me. I know what God says I deserve. Anything else is unacceptable and will not be tolerated."

Stan says, "Knowing my owner meant that I couldn't go against what He asked of me. What did He ask of me? To take care of my soul, the temple in which He lived. If anything should contaminate that temple—such as abuse—I needed to take distance from it."

Remo says, "It took a while because she had so much control over me, but I had to realize who I lived and died for—and it wasn't her. It was the One who made me, saved me and called me. Coming under His lordship left no room for her to control me."

Here's what those who STAYED within the relationship but broke free from toxic dynamics said:

Paul states: "My approval, value, acceptance and identity did not lean on my wobbly expectations of my wife but are anchored in the truth of who my Father says I am and knows me to be in plain view."

Vilma states: "As my relationship and dependence on God strengthened, I learned to continually turn to Him and lean on Him as my safe place and my shield. This meant I no longer had to turn to my own defenses and former methods of navigating toxic moments. I was able to hear and see the truth of how He saw me (His daughter, loved, protected, seen). As these truths took preeminence, the attempts that my spouse made to draw me into a power struggle were rendered ineffective.

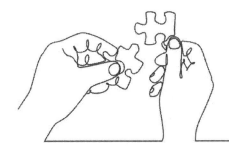

CHALLENGE

Putting the pieces together: The "Know Your Owner" Challenge.

- Set aside at least fifteen minutes each day for quiet time with God consisting of prayer, Bible reading and journaling.
- Get involved in a church community where you can glean from others' relationships with God.
- Serve God in some capacity that matches your abilities and aptitude within your church community.

CHAPTER TWELVE
Dodging Wild ASSES

"He will be a wild ass of a man; his hand will be against everyone,
and everyone's hand will be against him" (Genesis 16:12).

WILD ASSES

Wild ASSES are quarrelsome animals at war with everyone. Hence, the reason the scripture says, *"His hand will be against everyone."* Some might appear to have peaceful relationships but that's only because those particular associations remain superficial. Facts are, when you get up close and personal with a Wild ASS, you find out that contention is much more comfortable for them than concord. If you ever mate with a Wild ASS, you'll soon discover that you're continually baited into fights about the pettiest subjects. Mating with a Wild ASS involves endless competitions about who's smarter, sexier, stronger, and sweeter, etc. In the DSM-5 (Diagnostic and Statistical Manual of Mental Disorders, 5th Edition) one of the symptoms of narcissism—the clinical name for Wild ASS—is the insatiable need to feel superior over the other seven billion people on planet earth.

Sadly, these rivalries draw out the saddest parts of who you are. The longer you remain within these contentious relationships, the more unrecognizable you become to your own self. In the situation of Joel Steinberg and Hedda Nausbaum—a case of rivalry and domestic violence that ended in the murder of their six-year-old adopted daughter—Hedda finally morphed into a limp zombie from years of battering. Just as Winston Churchill stated, "Competition may bring out the best in product, but it also brings out the worst in men."

So the Wild ASS believes that everyone is at war with them, but so much of their perception is nothing more than projection, a theory of psychology whereby someone avoids certain unadmirable characteristics about themselves by attributing those characteristics to others. For instance, an angry person might strangely holler at you, "Stop being so angry!" Or a cheating spouse might accuse you of cheating. Projection happens when you spot in someone else a deplorable trait that *you* yourself have. It is like the guy who thinks that every room he enters stinks, when in fact the smell is coming from the dog poop under his own shoe. It is not uncommon for a Wild ASS to accuse you of attacking them when they are in fact attacking you. Yes, Wild ASSES believe that everyone is at war with them, but the truth is reverse—they are at war with everyone else.

If you've mated with a Wild ASS, you have probably wondered a million times, "How did he or she become like this?" In the backdrop of the passage above, the Wild ASS is a prophecy concerning Ishmael, a newborn baby abandoned by his father in the dangerous wilderness. According to Abraham Maslow, one of the most basic needs of a child that must be satisfied by caretakers is *safety*. When the need for *safety* is deprived by caretakers, the entire world becomes *unsafe*. Even those who wish them well are misconstrued as plotting, scheming and hiding an agenda.

Studies in neuroscience have shown that the brains of those with insecure relational attachments have an overactive amygdala. In other words, their fight/flight instincts are set-off much more than someone whose developed secure relationships early in life.

In fact, their brains perceive threat approximately 300 times more frequently when looking out at the world around them. Their lack of bonding with caretakers left them feeling unsafe with everyone. In short, the deprivation of safety needs during the formative years (in some way, shape or form) is typically the making of a Wild ASS.

**Wild ASSES are contentious animals
that will never COMPLETE you. Instead, all they
know how to do is COMPETE with you.**

Unleashed Fury

Remain guarded after your breakup with a Wild ASS because the fact that you are finished with them doesn't mean they are finished with you. A clean getaway from such malignant personalities is anomalous. More often than not, the abandonment they experience from the breakup unleashes a fury that's hard to handle. Wild ASSES are described as *wild* because of their erratic reactions to rejection. Below, you will notice a few different styles of fury they unleash; typically a Wild ASS will cycle back and forth between these styles.

1. Manipulation
In some cases, Wild ASSES endeavor to manipulate you back into their clutches—guilt trips, sympathy-solicitation or even charm. They may suddenly switch up from being a bully to playing the fragile victim that needs to be rescued. Be not deceived by these softer tactics. In time, you will discern that their charm is loaded with harm.

2. Accusations
When Wild ASSES realize they are no longer capable of controlling you, their final attempt to regain leverage is to control how others perceive you. It is not uncommon for their unleashed

fury to include false accusations against you, shaming you publicly on social media forums, slandering your character to important people in your life such as your children, your new boy/girlfriend or whomever is gullible enough to listen.

3. Intimidation

In the most extreme cases, Wild ASSES may resort to stalking, harassing phone-calls and letters, breaking and entering, destruction of property and even physical violence. Tragically, researchers Cooper and Smith (2011) reveal that one out of every five murder victims were killed by an intimate partner, many of who were exes. The purpose of sharing this statistic is not to make you *fearful* but *careful*. Wild ASSES are not miserable souls looking for company; rather, they are miserable souls who demand hostages.

4. Villainization

It is very common for Wild ASSES to villainize (treat like a villain) the very people they victimize. This villainization includes hating, blaming and waging war with you as if you're the one that hurt them. According to II Samuel 13, after Amnon attacks his half-sister Tamar, "he hated her."

Such audacity! The perpetrator actually hates the victim.

This villainization is a mechanism of the conscience whereby the Wild ASS avoids his own guilt by turning you into the bad guy/gal. Somewhere in the recesses of the Wild ASS's mind lingers the thought, "I have to make you terrible in order to make my actions against you tolerable."

Several years back, a team of psychologists recruited participants to administer electrical shocks on their fellow humanity.

They discovered that the more the participants administered the treatment, the less fondness they felt towards the people they shocked.

It can be inferred from this finding that we hate the people we hurt; and the more we hurt them, the more we hate them. Many victims of domestic violence attest to hearing their batterers say, "You made me do this!" with a rageful blame in their eyes.

Three muscles required
to dodge Wild ASSES

1. The Horn Muscle

As we stated earlier, an Ox's horn is used to protect itself from intruders; a metaphor of boundary enforcing.

Depending upon the severity of the Wild ASS's fury, you may have to enforce further boundaries in addition to the boundaries already established.

These boundaries might include blocking their calls, defriending and blocking them on social media, changing churches or other social institutions to avoid contact with them, restraining orders, no contact orders, etc.

Understand that firmness, not kindness, is the only proven tactic in managing furious Wild ASSES. Bullies only respect unwavering authority, not wishy-washy sympathy.

In the anointed words of St. Paul to the people of Galatia who were being pushed around by a controlling people known as the Judaizers: *"It is for freedom that Christ has set you free. STAND FIRM and do not let yourself be burdened again by a yoke of slavery"* (Galatians 5:1).

2. The Empathy Muscle

Exercising empathy is not the same thing as extending sympathy. As one poet described it, empathy is the power of perceiving the world through another's eyes. Empathy allows you to understand the situation in which Wild ASSES were groomed as well as recognize their present makeup. Empathy is exercised when the Wild ASS hurts you, you make an effort to understand their makeup rather than retaliate.

Empathy helps you escape from the resentment that bubbles up from an attack by a Wild ASS By empathizing with their limitations, it makes it easier to forgive *(don't confuse forgiveness with trust)* rather than resent them. Isn't it simpler to forgive a blind man for knocking over your vase than a man with sight? In the same way, Wild ASSES are emotionally handicapped, too blind to see how they hurt you. When you empathize with this limitation, you are less likely to be infected by the resentment that often ensues being wounded by Wild ASSES Jesus empathized with the Wild ASSES that nailed Him to the cross which made it possible to forgive them. Notice the second part of His statement which exemplifies empathy, *Forgive them for they do not know what they do" (Luke 23:34).*

3. The Ignore Muscle

Most of the unleashed fury of a Wild ASS is to be ignored. The Ignore Muscle is when you give no attention to the attacks against you. When Jesus was besieged by a mob of Wild ASSES, He used His ignore muscle. Consider I Peter 2:23, "Jesus did not retaliate when He was insulted, nor threaten revenge when He suffered. He left His case in the hands of God who always judges fairly." Of course, the Ignore Muscle is most difficult to use when you have been lied about or falsely accused. You will have to pray the words of St. Augustine, 'God, deliver me from my lust for vindication!'"

Once upon a time, an ornery dog woofed every morning at the rising of the sun. Every time the sun rose and started to shine brightly, the miserable dog went ballistic with his barking. Finally, the day came when the dog rolled over and died, but the sun kept shining! Let barking dogs bark while you just keep shining. Consider this promise stated in the Bible for those who trust in the Lord in the face of adversaries who malign them...

"He (God) will make your innocence radiate like the dawn,
and the justice of your cause will shine like the noonday sun"
(Psalm 37:6).

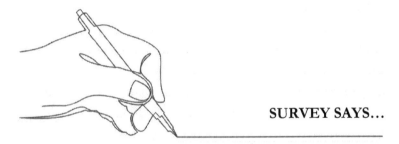

SURVEY SAYS...

Notes from our "Dodging Wild ASSES" survey:
Here's what those who LEFT the relationship said:

Ani states, "Probably the biggest backlash I dealt with from him was guilt-trips. We were both involved in the church, and he loved to send me messages loaded with Bible verses. Of course, Bible verses to use against me rather than a mirror for himself. He weaponized the Bible to make me feel like less of a Christian. But the more I learned the Word for myself, and found mercy from Jesus for my end of the deal, the less those guilt-trips worked. Oh, and then he also tried to destroy my reputation with his family."

Meg states, "Of course, he villainized me. I was the witch for *breaking up our family*. 'How could she do this to such a devout husband,' he would tell people. He could no longer control me, so he focused on controlling how others saw me. My response to this was using my ignore muscle. A refusal to participate in his games. I'm not going to lose my integrity by doing what he does to me."

Here's what those who STAYED within the relationship but broke free from toxic dynamics said:

Vilma says "We were both so verbally and emotionally abusive during arguments. I learned to leave if things were getting too heated. My husband did not respond well to this boundary many times and it needed to be reinforced over and over. It was the only way of dodging vicious toxic cycles."

Paul says, "I refused to participate in heated arguments. This often meant that the issues could not and would not be discussed immediately, even if my spouse demanded that. Often it would cause me to feel like I was abandoning her to her feelings while in essence I was creating a safer and stabler place for us to land."

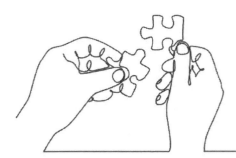

Putting the pieces together: The "Dodging Wild ASSES" Challenge.

- *The Horn Muscle.* Enforce necessary boundaries that match their fury. For instance, if the Wild ASS attacks you on social media, block him/her. If they threaten your life, file for a restraining order.
- *The Empathy Muscle.* Empathize with their situation. Once again, this does not mean extending sympathy. It simply means discerning their handicaps in order to forgive them for their cruelty.
- *The Ignore Muscle.* Keep Shining! Go after your goals while prohibiting the Wild ASSES from derailing you from your destiny.

CHAPTER THIRTEEN
Mate With Another OX

"The oxen were plowing while the asses were feeding behind them"(Job 1:14).

THE POWER OF SYNERGY

On a dog day afternoon in July, a rancher roots for his ox to haul a wheelbarrow out of a gulley. While the rancher banks on the astounding strength of the beast, he also knows the animal needs a little encouragement to get the job done. So he screams, "Come on Billy, pull that wagon! You got this, Johnny, tug that cart!"

Noticing the spectacle, a little boy stops to listen. Confused by what he hears, he remarks to the farmer, "Sir, why are you screaming two names when there's only one ox?"

The rancher smirks like a magician with a trick up his sleeve. He replies, "Why do I scream two names? If the Ox thinks he's alone, he's sure to quit before the job gets done. But if presumes he has a partner, there's no stopping him from accomplishing his mission."

Notice in Job 1:14, it's not an Ox plowing the field but Oxen; Ox is a single animal but Oxen refers to two or more Ox. Here, we see that the work is not accomplished alone but done with the support of a peer(s). In Deuteronomy 32:30, the author of the book, Moses, tells us that "one man chases a thousand while two men put ten thousand to flight." Basic arithmetic suggests that if one man chases a thousand, then two men could potentially pursue two thousand. One plus one equals two, right? When dealing with inanimate objects, this mathematical formula proves to be true. However, pertaining to living organisms such as animals and people, the combination of two produces a result exponentially larger than its predicted sum. This dynamic is known as, Synergy. According to Daniel Webster,

Synergy is the interaction of two or more agents to produce a combined effect greater than the sum of their separate effects.

Consider this concept as it applies to electricity. Why is a laser beam so much more powerful than a spotlight when they each have a similar number of photons? The spotlight will barely keep you warm while a laser beam could damage your pupil. A spotlight illuminates but a laser beam penetrates! The reason for the laser beam's power is that its photons aren't spread out in a hundred directions, isolated from one another like that of the spotlight. Rather, its photons lock together in agreement, and that synergetic relationship produces a result far greater than the sum of its separate effects.

All this to say, when God blesses you with a partner—a friend or a brother, a sister or a lover—He partners you up with someone to produce synergy. Given the fact that you are a social creature who feeds off of the feedback of others, the support of your partner inspires you to do more than you could ever do alone. Forging the right alliances will empower you to start a business, achieve a college degree, write a book, build a home or just become an overall better person.

Partnering up with the Right people produces synergy.

Traverse through the corridors of history and you will find that some of the greatest accomplishments were not the result of one person's energy, but two people's synergy. For instance, Microsoft was founded in 1975 by the synergetic genius of Bill Gates and Paul Allen. One of the trendiest ice cream shops of our era was established by two men known as Ben and Jerry. Even God when He created mankind in Genesis 1:26, He didn't say, "Let ME make man in My image." Instead, He said, "Let US make man in OUR image." As we see in this verse, the divine act of creation was a collaborative effort between the Father, the Son and the Holy Spirit.

Synergy is illustrated superbly in the friendship of two students from Chicago-Kent College of Law—Mr. Overton and Mr. Kaspryszak. Shortly after they met each other in school, the armless Kaspryszak guided the blind Overton through the stairways while the blind Overton carried the armless Kazpryszak's books. After they graduated, they made a plan to practice law together, believing that their partnership was not just sentimental but strategic. The mutual interdependence between Overton and Kaspryszak shows us how *team* work makes the *dream* work.

And of course, there's that famous scene from *Rocky 2*.

The champion hangs up his shorts and throws in the towel. He's all done with boxing.

He has no motivation whatsoever to return to the ring.

"Rocky!" his beloved wife, Adriane, says and beckons him to her side as she lays in a hospital bed.

"Win!" she whispers in his ear. The music plays while Rocky makes a sudden comeback to the gym!

This scene exemplifies the advantages of a man partnering up with the right woman.

The temptation to do it alone

Maybe you say to yourself, "I don't need anyone." Perhaps you're thinking, "I'm better off alone."

As much as you crave intimacy, you figured out that it usually doesn't come without some injury; therefore, in order to avoid the injury, you dodge intimacy. It is alarming—but not surprising—that a recent urban institute reported that seventy percent of millennials will be married by age forty, a dramatic dip from the ninety-one percent rate of Baby Boomers.

Before you settle for a companionless existence, notice something peculiar about the way God designed the human body. He made it physically unnatural to kick yourself in the butt or pat yourself on the back. Your body was fashioned in such a way that you need someone else to kick you in the butt or pat you on the back. Perhaps this was God's way of accentuating our need to have someone else correct us (kick us in the butt) or encourage us (pat us on the back). Maybe this was God's way of telling you that you would do far better in life by partnering up with someone than riding solo.

I'm not sure what Adam, the first man, was doing in Genesis 2:18, that God had to actually say, "It is not good for man to be alone…" I imagine Adam banging his head up against a tree, picking his nose to keep busy or shooting the breeze with some make-believe friends. In whatever way Adam was behaving, his conduct was so psychotic that it inspired God to say, "It ain't good for this brother to spend another minute alone!"

Research in neuroscience expounds upon the intensity of a chemical within our brain known as oxytocin. Neuroscientists dub this chemical, 'the bonding hormone' or 'the cuddling hormone' because it's a feel-good sensation that's released when we physically connect with someone.

The hormone is also known to reduce cortisol levels (a.k.a., stress) and improve our physical health on many levels. In light of these findings, it's no surprise that statistics reveal that single people live shorter life spans than married people. Why? Because, biologically, you require affection in order for your body to function. Just as the Bible says, "It is not good for man to be alone."

How do you know you have found an OX?

Let me offer you three litmus tests for determining whether you have found an OX. God forbid you should make the same mistake again by yoking with another ASS.

It is a fallacy to believe that people make a million mistakes in their lifetime. Facts are, people only make a handful of mistakes in their lifetime, but they make those same mistakes a million times. With that said, let's not be *fearful* but *careful* to choose wisely.

1. The HEALTHY Test

How spiritually and psychologically healthy are you right now? Are you wounded (based on the wounds mentioned in Chapter Ten), or are you whole?

The answer to these questions will determine the quality of the person you attract. Your vibe is what determines your tribe. If your vibe is toxic, then expect to attract toxic people.

If your vibe is healthy, then expect to attract healthy people. The first test has nothing to do with discerning the character of someone else but involves a thorough health evaluation of yourself. Quite simply stated, for as long as you act like an ASS, you are bound to attract ASSES. It's hard for us to face the fact that we are *attracting* how we are *acting*.

2. The ADVERSITY Test

In Chapter One, you were given the profile of an OX. Therefore, you know the characteristics to look for in someone before yoking with them. However, people in general are master impersonators. Folks pretend to be kind, generous and sacrificial all the time in order to woo someone into a relationship. As a pastor, I heard husbands and wives say many times, "My partner baited and switched up on me. When we dated, he/she was sweet. After we got married, they changed."

Truth be told, your partner didn't change; rather, the mask fell off. Therefore, you need enough time with that person to observe how they behave under adverse conditions.

Adverse conditions have a way of revealing what's truly inside of someone. If you plan on yoking with someone, you need the opportunity to watch how they behave under pressure, during conflict and within stressful circumstances. Adversity reveals character.

Let me break it down for you like this. Years ago, I was waiting on tables at a bistro while carrying a container of hot soup. A patron bumped into me, causing me to spill the soup everywhere. A person's true character is what spills out of them when life's circumstances bump into them.

3. The ENERGY Test

As we've witnessed throughout this book, a sure sign you've partnered up with the wrong person is that the relationship drains you. When you yoke with an ASS, the relationships will not *equip* you; instead, it *strips* you. If it were you in that classic scene from the movie, *Jerry Maguire*, you wouldn't say to your lover, "You complete me..." Instead, you would say, 'You deplete me!"

Conversely, relationships with other OXEN revitalize you. A strong indication that you have found an OX is when they inspire you to do better and be better.

You know you have found an OX when you make headway in various areas of your life rather than go in circles. A recent survey showed that the number one reason why people seek relationships, in addition to being loved, is to feel support.

In other words, we yearn for relationships with people who motivate us rather than relegate us.

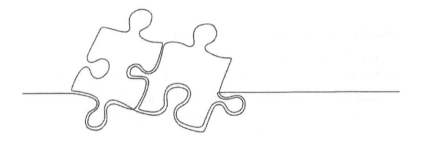

Conclusion

Notice in Job 1:14, the OXEN haven't gotten rid of the ASSES. While the OXEN plow together, the ASS is right beside them eating in the fields.

Facts are, you will never eliminate ASSES from your life.

You will collide with ASSES in the workplace.

You will bump into ASSES at the grocery market.

You will even sit next to ASSES on your committees, sports teams, support groups and other arenas of life.

A life without ASSES should not be the goal of a Christian, nor is it the objective of this book.

If a life without ASSES was a noble pursuit, Jesus would have never ate and drank with sinners, conversed with the Pharisees and even labored with some of his hard-headed, selfish disciples.

However, there is a vast distinction between the picture that Job paints in Job 1:14 and Moses alludes to in Deuteronomy 22:10. Within Job's picture, the ASS is an animal eating from the fields that the OX plows. Within Moses' picture, the ASS is an animal yoked to the neck of the OX. From God's standpoint, Job's picture is allowable whereas Moses' picture is intolerable. ASSES have a place in our life…behind us, feeding off of the virtues we exhibit. They may be your students, employees, acquaintances and even your children. But, as Moses states, ASSES have no place beside us, joined with a yoke as partners, lovers and intimate confidants.

May the ASSES be the people behind you whom you FEED, but God forbid the ASSES be the people beside you (yoked) whom you NEED.

About the Author

Michael A. Caparrelli, PhD (abd) served for sixteen years as a pastor of a recovery church in Rhode Island. Currently, he is in the final dissertation stage of his PhD in Behavioral Science, investigating the impact of church on the recovery journey of adults with addictions.

He travels across the nation, speaking to churches, schools, prisons and rehabs, on a variety of subjects in behavioral health from a faith-based perspective.

He also is an adjunct professor of psychology at Northpoint College and author of the well-received *Pen Your Pain Into Parables.*

He has four children—Ashley, Mikie, Hannah and Olivia. He is a devout follower of Jesus Christ.

If you would like to book Michael for a speaking engagement, please email him at: Michaelcaparrelli@unmuted.app

Acknowledgements

First and foremost, I give praise and thanksgiving to my Lord and Savior, Jesus Christ, for keeping me stable and productive during some very trying times.

To all of my mentors, my spiritual Father, Pastor Pat Manzo, my coach in the corner, Bishop Jeff Williams, my pastor, Tony Palow, the man who discipled me, Pastor Scott Axtmann and my business mentor and close friend, Matt Olerio, my spiritual moms, Jacqui Strothoff, Jen Tufano & Iris Pelley, you encouraged me beyond all of my insecurities and helped me find my dreams right on the other side of my fears.

To my children, Ashley, Mikie, Hannah and Olivia, allow God to map out your life, especially the picking of your mate. God knows what you desire and require far better than you do. I love and adore each of you, and you make my life complete.

To Joe Cannistraci, you were the one who invested in my spiritual formation when I was just a young Bible college student with not a penny in my pocket.

To John Stebbene, you saved my life this year and have always been a friend to lean on.

To my sweetheart Alicia, you are the OX who inspired this book. I love you and admire all of the virtues you so effortlessly exhibit.

And with thanks to:

Words in the Works for the production of this book:
www.wordsintheworks.com

Sarah Vass for the *OX and ASS* cover concept.

Rebecca Danielle and *Radiance by Rebecca Photography* at:
www.facebook.com/RRPhotography616/

Also by
Michael A. Caparrelli

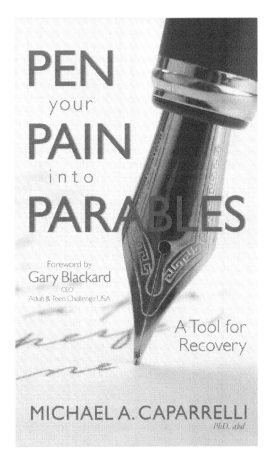

PEN
your
PAIN
into
PAR BLES

Foreword by
Gary Blackard
CEO
Adult & Teen Challenge USA

A Tool for
Recovery

MICHAEL A. CAPARRELLI
PhD, abd

Out of his own past along with a higher education in behavioral science, Michael A. Caparrelli, PhD (abd) helps you frame the painful moments of yours—the annoyances and the grievances, the losses and divorces, the abuse and the misuse, the rejection and depression—in a manner that transforms your story into the greatest asset you have.

By the end of *Pen Your Pain Into Parables*, you will no longer be emotionally crippled by the people, places and things of yesteryear. At one time, your past was an anchor that dragged you downward. After you pen your pain into parables, your past will become a rudder that guides them forward.

Accompanying workbook also available